MIND OVER MATTER

Dr Glen Barclay is Reader in History at the University of Queensland in Australia. His previous publications are *Twentieth Century Nationalism*, *Commonwealth or Europe?* and *Struggle for a Continent*. He has frequently broadcast on Australian radio on current affairs and historical subjects and has made a number of appearances in current affairs programmes on Australian television. His interests are literature, military history and the occult.

MIND OVER MATTER

Beyond the Bounds of Nature

GLEN BARCLAY

PAN BOOKS LTD

LONDON AND SYDNEY

First published in Great Britain 1973 by
Arthur Barker Ltd
This edition published 1975 by Pan Books Ltd,
Cavaye Place, London SW10 9PG

ISBN 0 330 24237 7

Made and printed in Great Britain by
Cox and Wyman Ltd, London, Reading and Fakenham

CONTENTS

Introduction: *what is going on?*

Anybody trying to discuss the kind of phenomena dealt with in this book faces two problems. The first is simply to find words for the concepts he is writing about. The second is to make them convincing to people who have not themselves shared any of the experiences referred to. Both these difficulties are of fairly recent vintage and are also confined to what one might conveniently lump together as the 'Western World'. Asian researchers on the occult have never been bothered in this way. Even in the West, educated people, at least until well into the eighteenth century, would have had no difficulty in accepting as an arguable proposition that the world of objective physical reality perceived by the senses of most people not obviously blind, deaf or insane, existed along with, and presumably originated from, another world not subject to the laws of physical nature; that the two worlds interpenetrated each other from time to time; and that by doing certain things or saying certain words, at certain times and certain places, individuals in the physical world could introduce into the affairs of the physical world forces which originated from the non-physical world. There might well be considerable disagreement about where these forces came from, and exactly how one summoned them from one world to another. But at least there were no difficulties about language. One was talking about people who called upon the Powers of Light or Darkness as the case might be, in order to conjure up good or, alternatively, evil spirits, which would give one a certain limited power to disregard the forces of Nature. It was all rather personalized, but there was no disagreement about the general idea.

Nor did the Victorians and their immediate successors have

much trouble with terminology, even in the full tide of progress
and self-confidence in the physical sciences. They merely
became more scientific themselves. Both the physical and non-
physical worlds were permeated by an omnipresent something
called the 'ether'. There was no vacuum for Nature to abhor,
and no annihilation to be afraid of. Man at least was an am-
phibious being, equipped with a physical body to inhabit the
physical world, and at least one etheric body to inhabit the non-
physical world. Communication between the two worlds was
achieved through making waves in the ether, as sound waves
are made in the air or the water in the physical world. Inhabi-
tants of the non-physical world revealed themselves to inhabi-
tants of the physical world through the process of
materialization, drawing on ectoplasm supplied from the body
of a receptive physical being called a medium. This could be
demonstrated by weighing mediums before and during mat-
erializations. The drawing off of ectoplasm by the intruding
spirit would cause the medium to lose some weight. It was all
very scientific, and is now coming back into fashion. It is just
that other terms are used.

The trouble is that none of them is very satisfactory. The
term 'psychic phenomena' necessarily bears a connotation of
spiritualistic seances, and communication with the dead, which,
at least on the face of it, has nothing to do with what we are
really concerned with here. What we are concerned with is
things done by living people which are unaccountable in purely
physical terms. 'Supernatural' has the same disadvantage of
connoting intervention by the dead, plus the additional objection of being logically meaningless. If a thing exists at all, it
necessarily exists in nature. It may be unfamiliar, or uncom-
mon, or physically unaccountable, or even an hallucination, but
it has either been experienced or it has not, and if it has been it
is part of nature, and not more than nature or less than nature.
In any case, the whole argument of contemporary research into
this area of experience is that the forces being examined, if they
exist at all, are not unnatural in any sense of being abnormal,
but are indeed inherent in the human make-up. The Victorians

were right to at least this extent. Man is an amphibian. It is part of his nature to have powers which are not wholly subject to physical limitations.

This argument similarly rules out words like the fashionable 'paranormal'. One cannot really talk sensibly about human qualities being more or less than normal. One can say only that they are present in some people in a more developed or effective form than in others.

The most convenient and adaptable term is certainly 'occult'. It is less loaded than its synonyms 'psychic' or 'mystic', because it implies only that the forces we are concerned with are not fully known, and there can be no argument about that. It is not known to everybody's satisfaction that they even exist. It is certainly not known where they come from, how they operate, how they are cultivated, and what they can do. What is known is that there is multiplying evidence, an increasing amount of it being derived from experiments carried out under unimpeachable laboratory conditions, that an enormously greater number of people than could have been suspected are doing things which were certainly generally believed to be physically impossible. They are also doing them to order, at the command of their own wills, and not as the result of any appeal to any notoriously unpredictable external factor, such as divine intervention. They may not exactly be doing it themselves, but at least they are acting as the agents through which it is being done. There are of course usually religious overtones, such as preliminary meditation, and the honouring of Taoist or Buddhist symbols, simply because such behaviour seems appropriate in the presence of what is, after all, still unknown; but there is no reason at all to believe that the rituals or incantations of what might be called orthodox western religion have the faintest bearing on the results achieved – even when the person responsible for the phenomena is himself a member of the Society of Jesus, as in the case of Father Gonzalez-Quevado, director of the Centro Latino-Americano de Parapsicologia at São Paulo, Brazil, the scene of the most astounding demonstrations of mind over matter ever publicly witnessed.[1]

It may seem surprising that the evidence of these fascinating phenomena has not been more systematically examined than it has been. The reason for this is quite simple. It has taken place to by far the greater extent in the particular and mundane field of unarmed combat, and scientists and parapsychologists in the West at least are not more noted for their interest in the martial arts, than devotees of unarmed combat are normally interested in science and parapsychology. It is also true that the combat arts which claim to develop occult powers are also to a great extent secret arts, cultivated by the most suspicious people on earth, the Chinese. The natural result is that these arts have developed in an almost impenetrable fog of confusion, ambiguity and obscurity, some accidental but a very great deal deliberate. The fog is not quite impenetrable, however. It is certainly possible to list more than enough examples of the physically impossible things which Asian students of martial and related arts claim to be able to do through the exercise of their mental powers. It is even easier to discover the very precisely described techniques by which they claim to acquire these powers. It is perfectly possible to find instances where these techniques or these claims have been tested or otherwise confirmed by laboratory or comparably reliable experiments. It is even possible at the end to make some kind of coherent pattern out of the truly bewildering variety of ideas and processes which we will find in the study of oriental occultism. The effort is well worth making. At the worst, one can expect to pick up a few useful hints on self-defence. At the best, one might learn to draw in some measure on the forces of another universe.

1 Secrets of self-defence:
western boxing, savate, jiu-jitsu, judo

It might well seem more than a little incongruous for a study of mystical or occult powers to be concerned at all with man's crudest and apparently most physical activity, fighting other men with his bare hands. The fact is however that the application of occult powers to what is hypocritically called the art of self-defence, is by far the best documented and most easily verifiable aspect of the exercise of mind over matter. There can be little doubt as well that it is perhaps the most intrinsically interesting as well as certainly the most confusing part of an area of study, most of which is interesting, and nothing at all about which is simple. It is also in some ways the most revealing. The methods of certain styles of the martial arts developed in parts of Asia are based on principles which not only reject completely any merely materialistic view of how the universe works, but also (and far more significantly) explain in the most precise manner possible just how non-physical forces can be cultivated and directed to achieve very basic physical ends, like injuring one's opponent without risk to oneself. All one has to do is decide whether the principles and techniques have any real validity. The problem is as always one of trying to find out if anything is really happening.

In one sense, this association of physical combat with the occult is really only natural. It responds to one of the most fundamental of all human concerns. The most popular human wish would presumably be to live forever in the universe we are already acquainted with. Little less popular, however, would be the wish to be able to defeat one's enemies without undue risk to oneself. This aspiration has of course inspired the enormous and ever-increasing list of invulnerable heroes chronicled in pulp fiction and comics, who fight and never lose because they can always fall back on some paranormal faculty which the bad guys can never match. Hence the procession of wish-fulfilment monsters, supermen, rubbermen, sharkmen, spidermen, invisible men, amazing men, steel skulls and the like, epitomized in Gerald Kersh's glorious conception of Ironskin Ormsk. There can be no doubt about the fervour of the human desire to identify with an invulnerable champion and if possible acquire some of his invulnerability. What is more surprising is that western culture, which has produced the martial arts fantasies of the comic strip, has itself produced in practice only utterly prosaic and indeed generally discredited forms of combat, with no mystical pretensions whatever. Occult combat exists only in Asia, if it can be shown to exist at all.

It is not necessary to suggest reasons why this should be the case, but it is not difficult either. There is the overall general consideration that Asian ways of life and thought are more congenial to mysticism in its various forms than European ways are. There is also the fact that the Christian religion in Europe has for most of its existence been concerned with frustrating, disappointing and generally discouraging the physical body, rather than with developing its higher powers, even if it was admitted that it could have any. It was thus quite appropriate that physical combat should have been associated in Asia with monasteries and schools of philosophy, and in Europe with the least religious or philosophical elements of society.

This was indeed not the case entirely while the concept of Chivalry remained significant in Europe. Chivalry linked the profession of arms with the notion of religious consecration. It was, however, still a religion which tended to regard the manifestation of occult powers as proof of diabolical possession. Legends of paranormal fighting prowess in chivalrous Europe tended to attribute occult powers to weapons, rather than to the men using them. No mystical flavour lingered on in any case to give glamour to the European arts of unarmed combat. These were in fact surprisingly late to develop, simply because few people tended to go about unarmed until the eighteenth century. This was true not merely of the nobility. Walter Scott's Highland Drover complained bitterly to the Englishman who wanted to beat him up, that serious fighting was done with the blade. Various schools of wrestling and fist fighting had of course developed from the earliest times, but essentially for exercise or entertainment, for the gymnasium or the arena, rather than the street or the battlefield.

Western boxing

All this was hardly altered at all by the phenomenal growth of English boxing as by far the most widely known form of self-defence in the world. Boxing developed from a sport into a business. Its success was due primarily to its appeal as a spectacle, to its apparent simplicity and to the fact that professional boxing offered a prospect of making a great deal of money very quickly to people who lacked the ability or the opportunity to make any sort of a living any other way. It had, in other words, exactly the same kind of appeal as crime, with the added advantage that it made fewer mental demands on its practitioners, even if its physical demands were usually more excessive. Sadly, most young men who adopted professional boxing as a living would probably have enjoyed healthier and more prosperous lives as housebreakers, pickpockets or standover men. Even more sadly for the honour of the profession, the connection between boxing and crime has become all too apparent. It is not merely the case that organized crime has traditionally interested itself in the 'fixing' of profitable fights. The fact is also that the unsuccessful or ageing boxer may well find himself unqualified for any legal way of earning a living outside the ring. Dr Philip J. Rasch accordingly denounced as 'a simplistic and dangerous generalization ... [without] the *slightest* validity' what he calls 'the British reverence for the sport and its practitioners', as shown in the statement in a recent book on self-defence that 'the gentlemen of the ring who are skilled in boxing confine their skill to the sport'.[1]

Western boxing has thus developed in a climate about as unmystical as any that could well be imagined. This is not to say that it has not acquired its legends and mysteries. On the simplest and most basic level, there is the difficulty of relating punching ability to any recognizable combination of physical or mental qualities. It is certainly true that some of the hardest hitters of modern times have been among the most impressively developed boxers, from the physical culturists' point of view, such as Joe Louis, Max Baer or Muhammad Ali. It is also true that some of them have been among the least physically impressive, such as Bob Fitzsimmons, Al Hostak or the Australian Jack Hassen. There have also been men of overwhelming physique like Al Simon, Bruce Woodcock or Joey Maxim, who have simply not punched with anything like the effectiveness which their muscularity would suggest. Nor does the quality of viciousness usually termed the 'killer instinct' explain this discrepancy. Some of the most terrific hitting in the ring has been achieved consistently by courteous and amiable gentlemen like Archie Moore, Henry Cooper and Rocky Marciano, while some of the most socially irresponsible brawlers like Harry Greb, Billy Papke or Billy Conn have had to wear their opponents down by the cumulative effect of comparatively light punches.

None of this necessarily calls for occult explanations. Nor perhaps do extraordinary displays of individual skill by western boxers, such as the ability of the Australian Albert Griffiths ('Young Griffo') to evade punches while standing on a handkerchief, even when old, grossly overweight, drunk and apparently stupid. There is also the persisting mystery of the 'corkscrew punch' of Kid McCoy, which undoubtedly existed, as his victims testify, but which no other boxer has ever successfully explained or copied. There is no question that western boxing is a far more complex and obscure activity than is usually appreciated. On the other hand, one must admit that the only western boxer of note who ever actually claimed occult powers was Lou Nova, who claimed to be studying yoga in preparation for his fight with Joe Louis; who predicted success for himself through the operation of a 'cosmic punch' which he had acquired from the practice of yoga; and who in the end fought, quite understandably, one of the most hesitating and uninspiring, as well as unsuccessful fights of his career against Louis. Muhammad Ali also attributed his one-round knockout of Sonny Liston to a 'karate punch'; but there is little occult about karate, and in the opinion of many critics, Liston was beaten before he ever stepped into the ring.

What these facts do illustrate is that western boxing has many very serious limitations as a form of self-defence. It is for example unique among self-defence techniques in having no formal system of defence. The western boxer relies for protection on his ability to duck or slip punches; to cushion them on his arms, the palms of his hands or relatively insensitive parts of his body and above all to hit his opponent first. The eastern concepts of blocking and parrying are scarcely taught in western boxing, and have scarcely been used, except by a few isolated masters like Larry Gans, Tommy Burns and Jack Johnson. The result is of course that one repeatedly sees even the most skilful western boxers, like Ali, Fred Apostoli or Lionel Rose being hit by the wildest and longest of punches, because their hands and arms did not happen to be in the right place to receive them.

This defensive weakness arises, like all the other weaknesses of western boxing, from the fact of its being above all else a sport. Punching is spectacular. Blocking is not. More seriously still boxing, being a sport, is performed according to certain rules and subject to certain limitations which have exactly the same relevance to actual combat as the hunter's code, that one should never shoot a sitting bird, and should shoot a flying one only in the season. Boxing is thus based on the assumption that in any fight one will be wearing padded gloves; will be naked to the waist, or at most be wearing a singlet; and will not be allowed to deliver, and therefore will not have to guard against, blows delivered below the waist, or delivered to any part of the body except with the clenched knuckles. The effect of the glove is all-important here. The boxer is not in reality hitting with his knuckles at all. He is hitting with a blunt instrument,

The effect of his blows will therefore depend not on focusing
for penetration, but on the speed and weight he can put behind
the wide surface of the glove which will be coming in contact
with his opponent's body. Hence the western boxer, again
unlike any other self-defence exponent, delivers his most
effective blows in a rolling motion, punching with a horizontal
fist across his body, following through like a tennis player or
golfer. He is also relying for both attack and defence on qualities of speed of reaction, sense of timing and physical durability which can hardly be taught in any real sense, which can
only be innate, and which he will inevitably lose very quickly
indeed as he passes his athletic peak, sometime in his late
twenties.[2]

One must not of course discredit western boxing unwisely.
Its emphasis on speed, evasion and economy of movement must
place it among the fastest, most unpredictable and therefore
most likely to be effective among the fighting arts, when employed by an expert who has time to get his hands up. However,
its basic artificiality, its limited range of responses, its almost
total lack of anything that could be called system, the fact that
it relies for its successful operation upon skills that cannot
really be taught to anybody who does not possess them naturally, and above all the fact that it can be used effectively only
by the most athletic, all come close to disqualifying it as a
fighting art at all. It is best described as a spectacular and
tolerably efficient way of inflicting injury. The fact is that the
old pre-Queensberry styles of the London Prize Ring were
probably far more realistic methods of self-defence. They at
least employed a rigid guard across the vulnerable centre of the
body, used mainly straight punches to achieve the maximum
impact with bare knuckles and incorporated techniques of
grappling with and throwing an opponent.

Savate

On the other hand, the most practically effective of all the
fighting arts which does not pretend to occult powers, and the

only western system of self-defence which is incontestably superior to its Asian counterparts, French boxing or savate, utilizes the efficient body mechanics of orthodox English boxing, but employs punches mainly as feints to prepare the way for the serious business of kicking. Savate is at once immensely systematized, highly and deliberately artistic, extremely secret and a most reassuring thing with which to be familiar.

All this explains why the western consciousness was so receptive to the techniques of the Asian martial arts, which began to reveal themselves in successive waves after the turn of the century. The non-athletic, the intellectual and the cowardly were all prone to be interested in any system of self-defence which did not depend entirely upon brute strength and physical courage. It was in any case a time when western spiritualism and eastern occultism or esotericism combined to stimulate men's minds with notions of new universes or at least new dimensions to the present one. Anything out of Asia was expected to be mysterious and hoped to be enlightening. There was no doubt that the Asian martial arts were satisfactorily mysterious. They began obscure, and became more so. Some eighty years later, we are still trying to agree on how they actually work.

Jiu-jitsu

It cannot be repeated too often that one of the primary reasons for this obscurity is the basic one of language. Asian languages are enormously evocative and symbolic; Asian writers use symbols with more enthusiasm than precision; and European translators frequently misunderstand the symbols or mix them up. Nothing could show this more clearly than the western response to the first of the oriental martial arts to be introduced outside Asia, the highly basic and rough-and-ready Japanese system of jiu-jitsu. The confusion arose from the name. 'Jiu' has in Japanese the sense of 'yielding' or 'submission'. These concepts have in the West the connotation of softness or gentleness. Jiu-jitsu thus became customarily known in the West as 'the

way of gentleness', and regarded as an essentially non-violent,
passive means of responding to an attack by using in some
mysterious way the strength of the assailant against himself.

This, however, was all wrong. The Japanese term was actually intended to symbolize the notion of the 'submission throw',
at that stage still unfamiliar in western wrestling, in which one
goes in the same direction as the force being applied by an
attacker, thereby breaking his balance. There is no notion of
'gentleness' about the technique at all. It is in any case only one
of the methods incorporated in the general *mélange* of jiu-
jitsu, most of the techniques of which are disconcertingly
straightforward and unyielding.[3] The idea of 'gentleness'
becomes still more ridiculous when one realizes that jiu-jitsu
was never intended to be a self-sufficient system of unarmed
self-defence in the first place: its proper function was that of an
adjunct to the use of arms by a samurai, in a situation where he
might not be willing or able to get his sword out in time to deal
with an adversary that way. Its function was thus exactly that
of the very similar techniques of disarming an opponent taught
in the Italian schools of fence in the eighteenth century: they
were not to be employed as a substitute for weapons, but to
support their use.[4]

All this of course was utterly ignored by the enthusiastic
western pupils of the Japanese masters. What seemed to be
important was that jiu-jitsu provided a thoroughly comprehensive system of self-defence techniques, available for use
in any imaginable emergency, and apparently not dependent
for their success on the physical strength or durability of the
person using them. The interest naturally lay in trying to find
out what these techniques really were dependent on. There was
any amount of room for speculation. One reason for their un-
doubted success in demonstrations against western boxers and
wrestlers was clearly simply the factor of surprise. There was
nothing mysterious about submission throws, wristlocks and
strangles applied by grasping a person's collar, except that respectable western boxers and wrestlers were proscribed from
using these methods according to the rules of their respective

sports, and consequently did not expect to have to deal with them. They were not so mysterious to the muggers of the underworld. On the other hand, the technique of striking at or applying pressure to certain vulnerable spots or 'nerve pressure-points' certainly indicated a knowledge of physiology on the part of the orientals which was not only far greater than anything met with among western fighters, but which also appeared at times to be based on ideas about the nature of the human body and its powers which were actually different from those of western science. In the same way, the preference for circular motion when striking, parrying or grappling was also quite different from the relatively straightforward motions of western combat, and was not always clearly related to simple concepts of body mechanics. It was, in other words, not always possible to find reasons which made sense in material terms for the way the Japanese masters moved.

Unfortunately, it was not possible to get any satisfactory answers to these questions from the Japanese themselves. The regrettable fact was that jiu-jitsu was really a very unphilosophical and down-to-earth method of combat by oriental standards. It was above all unsystematic. It was also on the way out. It was, in fact, of fairly recent vintage, having been developed in the Sengoku and Tokugawa periods, between 1477 and 1868, for use by samurai in circumstances where they did not happen to be using their swords. It had never been more than a rag-bag of combat techniques, which clearly drew upon other and more systematic styles still unknown to the world at large, but which had never been organized into a coherent system itself. There were indeed some 725 officially recognized different schools of jiu-jitsu extant at the time of the Meiji restoration, which guaranteed the decline of this method of combat by bringing the rampages of the samurai to an end. They were no longer in occupation. Jiu-jitsu had become mainly a public amusement by the 1870s, rather than a serious system of self-defence. It has never really recovered, although it remains the basic system of unarmed combat taught to oriental police forces.

This could be considered a pity in many ways. Jiu-jitsu always possessed the primary recommendation for any combat art: it was effective, at least in the hands of someone who knew what he was doing. It comprised naturally some of the best methods of a multitude of other, more esoteric arts: it incorporated the turning movement of aikido, the foreknuckle strike and simultaneous parry of Chinese boxing, along with the incomparably simple and reliable wristlock of tai-chi ch'uan, applied by exerting pressure in opposing directions against an opponent's wrist and elbow, the nearest approach to an infallible combat method that exists. Its trouble has always been literally that it combines too many good things. There is no standard jiu-jitsu response available for all situations. There is no automatic sequence of movements which one can fall into spontaneously. Learning jiu-jitsu is, in other words, uncommonly like learning Japanese. One has to remember an enormous variety of moves and postures, not necessarily related one to another. There is no doubt that jiu-jitsu was most effective when used by the people for whom it was intended, by samurai who could always fall back on their trusty swords if they happened to have forgotten the next move.

Judo

Jiu-jitsu did nonetheless raise certain questions, which in a fairly modest way called into question a materialistic or mechanistic concept of the universe. Far more questions were raised by a far more popular and far more ineffective art, designed precisely to supplant jiu-jitsu as a popular sport, rather than as a system of unarmed combat. Jigoro Kano first introduced judo as a sport in Tokyo in 1882, with nine students. There are now a reputed 500,000 Black Belts in the world. His enormous success was due to a very simple formula: he eliminated the danger and accentuated the mystery. Kano quite deliberately removed the techniques from jiu-jitsu which could inflict injury upon a person before he had a chance to submit, such as blows, kicks, hairpulls, and all manner of attacks upon the so-

called 'pressure-points'. These fighting methods were to be
made available only to advanced students who had proved that
they possessed the appropriate spiritual qualities. What was
left was a system of grappling, in which the primary objective
was to throw the opponent off-balance, or secure his submission
by applying a stranglehold or pressure to the joints from which
he could obtain relief only by surrendering.

This was, however, quite genuinely the less important part of
judo. The most important was undoubtedly what might be
called the spiritual side. Judo masters introduced into their
schools or *dojos* methods of physical training apparently bor-
rowed from yoga and other eastern systems of spiritual development, in which the adept practised certain physical
postures for the sake of their spiritual effects. Meditation
became recognized as an essential part of training. So was
standing on one's head. So to a less urgent extent was some
acquaintance with the Japanese language, and preferably some
skill in Japanese calligraphy. For almost the first time at all,
and certainly for the first time on any extensive scale, the West
was being introduced to the oriental concept of using physical
exercises to acquire powers which were not obviously related to
any physical basis.

This of course was something totally different from the
Christian concept of self-torture in order to destroy one's
bodily aspirations. It was not just that the flagellant or faster is
trying to feel pain, while the yogi is trying not to feel pain. It
was rather that the Christian ascetic was trying to demolish his
body, while the oriental occultist was trying to use his to acquire powers which admittedly might reduce his dependence on
his bodily resources. This was quite explicit in the way of judo.
The judoka's physical training was intended to produce two
distinct effects. On the one hand, the practices of unhurried
movement, of quietness within the dojo, of bodily relaxation
and immobility, and above all of meditation kneeling Japanese-
style or sitting cross-legged with erect spine but depressed
shoulders, were supposed to induce a perpetual mood of
calmness, indifference to danger or the prospect of pain,

detachment, relaxation and inoffensiveness, combined with a
capacity for instant appropriate physical response to attack. On
the other hand, the advanced judoka undisguisedly owed his
unbreakable calm to powers which appeared to go considerably
beyond normal athletic skills. It was not just that he could
count on his superior knowledge of body mechanics to be able
to break even the strongest opponent's balance, and thus render
him helpless. He also expected to have acquired a sensitivity in
combat situations which amounted to telepathy or precognition. A judoka did not need strength or even speed in any
normal sense, because he could always get out of the way of an
attack. He could get out of the way because, being perfectly
calm himself, his mind undistracted by fear or aggressive
emotion, he could always sense when an assailant was about to
make his move, and apply the appropriate counter.

These qualities stemmed from the supposed Buddhist
origins of judo. It was at least true that judo was based on other
systems which very definitely purported to draw on occult resources by techniques of Buddhist meditation. There was also
no doubt that a great many people, by no means all judoka,
were prepared to take on trust the claims of what had started
off as only a Japanese spectator sport, after all. Nor was there
any question about the brilliant and humiliating successes
which individual judoka were able to gain in bouts with west-
ern-style boxers and wrestlers. Even more convincing were the
occasional victories won by judoka against muggers and brawlers in street or bar. Judo began to acquire a legend of invulnerability more complete than that surrounding any other
fighting art, before or since. It became the basis for the unarmed combat techniques taught to soldiers in western armies
from 1908 on. But the picture was not entirely satisfactory.
In the first place, there was always some difficulty in recognizing the traits of the ideal judoka in any practitioners of
the art whom one actually met. Some were reasonably
calm and serene, others notably less so. It was also reasonable
to suspect both that much of this serenity derived from their
belief that they were invulnerable in physical combat, and

that this belief had a rather unsatisfactorily narrow basis in reality.

To begin with, the bouts arranged between judoka and western boxers and wrestlers were almost never satisfactory, simply because good boxers and wrestlers, which meant professional boxers and wrestlers, were simply not going to risk their own reputations, which meant their own earning power, by taking part in combats with people who would not be fighting according to the rules. The fact is of course that even the argument over the relative merits of boxing and wrestling has never been settled satisfactorily, because no good boxer has ever agreed to fight a good wrestler since Gotch threw Frank Slavin out of a ring seventy years ago. Apart from anything else, there is the technical difficulty that such a bout would have to be fought under a new set of rules, in which the boxer would have to be allowed to wrestle and kick, and the wrestler to fight with his fists if he wanted to. Even the successes of the judoka in street brawls were not always a convincing proof of the supremacy of their art, since their best victories owed everything to the element of surprise. In any case, an experienced fighter in any combat style will usually beat a person who is experienced in none, and few muggers have had the time to become skilled fighters in any style.

But the main trouble with judo, even at the height of its popularity, was two-fold. In the first place, it was even less systematic than jiu-jitsu. The avoidance of punishing blows or holds meant that efforts were concentrated entirely on breaking the opponents' balance, and there were a multitude of ways in which this could be done, none notably more effective than any other. Nor did judo follow any unchanging pattern of body mechanics, as jiu-jitsu had done. Jiu-jitsu either punched or turned. Judo pushed, pulled, tripped, twisted and could become terrifyingly hard to remember. Even when there were usually only three separate movements in each judo counter, none of the three was likely to follow as a natural sequence from another. Applied to actual self-defence situations, this complexity could become stark lunacy. A woman seized by the wrist might for example be advised in a judo handbook on self-defence to grasp the assailant's little finger with her free hand (first movement); apply pressure against the joint until she had prised his hand loose (second movement); take her opponent's wrist with both hands (third movement); raise his arm (fourth movement); turn her back on him (fifth movement); pull his arm over her shoulder (sixth movement); and throw him (seventh movement).[5] It would of course be virtually certain that she would never be allowed to finish even the first movement, let alone any of the further ones necessary to complete the response. Even if she had been able by some miracle to finish the routine, there would still be the problem of what to do with the assailant after she had thrown him. By contrast, any classical oriental system of self-defence would prescribe exactly one movement: hit him in the eyes or the obliques hard enough to blind him or paralyse him. Then run.[6]

Judo was not really practical. No system of combat which actually tries not to injure the assailant can be. But the annoying thing was that judo masters also claimed to know methods, called *atemi*, which were quite devastating, quite mysterious, and only to be made available to the elect. The conclusion was therefore inescapable that if one knew what these methods were, one would have no need to spend years learning the multitudinous, elaborate and unsafe methods of conventional judo. It was only a matter of time before some enterprising Japanese would come along to lift the veil on the systems of truly destructive self-defence which the judo masters had to their credit attempted to keep obscure. In doing so, the teachers of the new art raised the veil on something else. Jiu-jitsu had hinted at mysteries and raised disturbing questions; judo had made pretensions to the occult or at least the superhuman, without convincingly substantiating them; the new arts brought back the realm of magic. People began openly and in the most mundane way to do things which simply set aside physiological reality. Human flesh was seen to be harder than wood, brick or stone; skin did not bleed when cut; a man could exert through his little finger greater power than six others could exert with their whole bodies. Something really quite extraordinary was happening. Either the occult existed and was within the physical reach of mankind, or there were even more dupes and liars around than the sceptics had bargained for.

2 At the portals of the supernatural: *karate, kiai-jutsu, shorinji kempo*

Karate

Karate was always the ultimate art of violence lurking behind the gentle façade of judo. Karate was *atemi*. Judo might be the soft way, karate was the hard way. Judo used wherever possible the force of the enemy against himself, karate opposed his force with greater or more effective force of one's own. Judo used grappling methods almost entirely, karate relied almost completely on blows with fists, knees, feet, elbows, head and any other part of the body which might be employed for that purpose, using grips and holds only to immobilize an opponent's striking arm, while one got on with the serious business of beating him to a jelly. This situation of contradicting methods of course brought one immediately up against the dilemma found throughout the study of the martial arts, that if the principles on which one particular art is based are right, then those of another art must simply be wrong. One might try to get out of the difficulty by suggesting that judo and karate were only different ways of reaching the same goal, but it was still disconcerting to note that the fundamental methods of one way were simply incompatible with those of the other.

Karate was and remains simply the art of bringing the greatest possible physical force to bear upon an opponent in the most damaging way possible. American professional teachers of karate have by now succeeded in corrupting and debasing the art from what had been a totally stylized and logically coherent form of combat, to utterly chaotic and unprincipled roughhousing. One characteristic of the art at least has endured, however: the karateka usually blocks and nearly always hits in a manner which develops the maximum straightforward impact. That is to say, the karateka still fights characteristically in a 'stop-go' fashion, involving three distinct movements, albeit applied with sometimes phenomenal speed. He has to be fast if his art is to work at all. The blocking hand or arm is driven against the attacker's arm, sometimes straight from wherever it happens to be, but sometimes after having been first withdrawn to generate greater momentum; the other hand not in use is drawn back, usually to the hip; and the counter-attack is launched by sending the withdrawn hand straightforwardly to its target, at the same time withdrawing the blocking arm to the hip. It is perhaps worth mentioning that the legendary karate chop is probably the form of attack least frequently used in karate, and may generally be dismissed as the most useless of all forms of attack, except against an opponent who is either blind or has his hands tied behind his back. The normal karate response is a straight punch, in the performance of which the wrist is turned so that the knuckles of the fist are horizontal at the moment of impact. It is another principle that the opposite leg should be advanced at the time of delivery, although one can step forward while actually punching.

As an indication of the impossibility of ever being able to say anything unreservedly about any of the martial arts of Asia, it is worth mentioning that in the most functional forms of Chinese boxing, which seem on every test to be far more practically effective than karate, the punch is usually delivered with the knuckles vertical, not horizontal; the distance between fist and target is as short as possible, not as long; the leg on the side of the punching hand, is advanced, not withdrawn; and blocking and punching are done simultaneously, not alternately. Once again, one finds completely incompatible principles in the same art.

Karate obviously had enormous attractions. In the first place, it was conspicuously simpler than judo. There are of course an immense variety of strikes and blocks in the karateka's armoury, but the techniques of performing them were at

least initially inflexible and easily comprehended. Con-
ventionally, the left arm went up to block, and the right arm
and leg went back. Then the right arm went forward to strike,
the right leg went forward with it, and the left arm and leg went
back. It could not unfairly be said that karate appealed to
simple minds. So, naturally, did the rigidity and tenseness of
the movements and the unconcealable emphasis on violence. It
was not perhaps the fault entirely of the Japanese that karate
was normally offered in the western press as a destructive form
of self-defence, enabling one to kill a man with one's bare
hands. However, it was inevitable that this should be the case,
given two of the most characteristic features of the Japanese
art. These were first of all the importance attributed to breaking bricks, tiles and planks of wood with the hardened hands,
and secondly, the screams and grimaces with which the movements of karate were carried out.

These were also the features of karate which most impressed
the West. It was literally appalling to discover that there were
men who could break up to thirty roofing tiles with their bare
knuckles, rather more with the sides of their hands, and some-
what fewer with their heads. It was understood initially that
one acquired the ability to do things like this by toughening the
striking surfaces of one's body by hitting them against coils of
rope tied tightly around a wooden pole. The physiological explanations of what happened next tended to differ, but the ultimate objective was to develop callouses over the striking
areas, which would be both insensible to pain, and also cushion
the impact on bone surfaces beneath the striking areas, to prevent fracture. It was also discovered that repeated blows with
the knuckles against an unyielding surface would cause the
bones themselves to increase in size, becoming swollen and
pointed, in contrast to the soft and protected knuckles of a
western-type boxer, which become swollen and flat, or
rounded.

Nothing less mystical than this could possibly be imagined.
Limited imagination and insensitivity to pain indeed appeared
to rank high on the list of required qualities for a karate master.

American gymnasium proprietors cashed in on the new boom by converting themselves into black belts over a period of weeks by hammering their knuckles out of shape on any convenient hard surface. Scientific skills were indeed cultivated. Articles were published, listing the most fragile woods and the most brittle bricks for use in public exhibitions of plank-breaking and brick-smashing. It was all very uninspiring.

But this circus atmosphere was obviously only part of the story. Japanese karate masters at least had always insisted on the vital importance of at least potentially occult elements like meditation and correct breathing. Karate was linked intimately with Zen Buddhism, as indeed were the other Japanese martial arts. Meditation was supposed to produce an attitude of mindless awareness, in which the karateka would respond spontaneously and without reflection to any situation which called for the exercise of his art, uninhibited by any emotion towards his opponent, any concern for victory or any anxiety about the consequences of defeat for himself. This mood of tranquil detachment was a little hard to discover in the yelling and smashing atmosphere of karate dojos. But it was evident from the start that the yellers and smashers were frequently doing things which were not obviously the result of simple crude physical effort.

The yell itself, or *kiai*, was a complex phenomenon. There were obvious counterparts in western experience. Wrestlers grunt, boxers snort and weightlifters puff, blow and groan. The simplest physiological excuse for this variety of noises is that they all have the effect of expelling stale air from the lungs, thereby causing a speedy intake of energizing oxygen. There are of course the further motivations of plain imitativeness, a desire to impress or alarm one's opponents, and the desire to gain a psychological release from fears of failure or personal injury, which might inhibit one from making a supreme effort. The noisy exhalation of air thus acts as an evocation of the basic animal in man, rejecting conventional social or rational restraints on his physical actions. It indicates that the person making the noise is no longer to be deterred by normal human doubts and fears. This aspect of the yell is seen most clearly in the image of the bayonet-charging soldier.

Another function of the *kiai* particularly relevant of the karateka is that it would anticipate and perhaps conceal any scream of pain that might be extracted from him, if the brick were to prove harder than his hand. At the same time, any observer of athletic contests could not fail to be aware that as a general rule, the better the boxer, the less notable his snorts; and the greater the weight being lifted, the less audible the groans of the lifter. It might also well be the case that the deadlier the bayonet fighter, the more silent and tightlipped might well be his approach. British commandos were not renowned for the amount of noise they made as they went into action. The probability had to be considered that one could perhaps hit as hard without the *kiai* as with it, if one really knew what one was doing.

But the trouble is that it is really very hard to know just what the smashers and yellers of karate are doing. It would be too much to expect that any aspect of the occult would ever be uncomplicatedly clear and logical. There are very compelling reasons to believe that there might be some power in the breath itself, or at least conveyed by it, quite distinct from any physical power being exerted by the breather. The concept of breath control is present as an integral part of yoga, as well as of the Asian martial arts, as if the breath were literally the channel through which occult forces of intrinsic energy operate in man. This aspect is dealt with more fully in succeeding chapters. However, it might be mentioned here that the notion is by no means unfamiliar even to conventional western mysticism: apart from the various activities attributed to the Holy Spirit ('Breath') there is the recorded action of Christ, when he breathed on the disciples after His resurrection to infuse them with occult powers.

There is also the extremely interesting and possibly useful advice given by Brian Fawcett, in his book *Operation Fawcett*,[1] where he explains how evil spirits can be routed by forcibly blowing wherever one senses their presence. It is admittedly usually difficult to know in normal circumstances whether one is being confronted by an evil spirit or not. However, there is no doubt that it is quite a normal experience to feel unaccountably apprehensive in certain circumstances, and equally no doubt that a session of hearty blowing infallibly dispels such feelings. *Experentia docet.*

Kiai-jutsu

More directly relevant here is no doubt the fact that there are schools of combat in Japan which claim to be able to achieve most impressive physical results with the use of the breath and perhaps the vocal chords alone. Their particular art is named 'kiai-jutsu' (spirit shout art). One is peculiarly harassed here by a lack of witnesses. However, there are at least two westerners who have testified to experiencing something quite extraordinary. John F. Gilbey* is naturally the most spectacular. He tells how he met by an extraordinary coincidence a Japanese practitioner of traditional medicine named Junzo Hirose. Mr Hirose explained that there was nothing superhuman about kiai-jutsu, although it required an innate talent, and that it was the perfect street-fighting technique, because it enabled the artist to kill or wound from a distance, thereby avoiding any chance of accidental injury to himself in a close-up brawl. Gilbey does not in fact say if Mr Hirose demonstrated his power to injure from a distance. However, he describes Hirose's power to cure or to paralyse. In the first case, Hirose struck an assistant in the face, making his nose bleed, then, after a pause of fifteen seconds or so, produced a terrifying roar, 'like a clap of thunder', coincident with which the bleeding stopped totally. He then invited Gilbey to attack him, and apparently stopped him in his tracks, probably producing temporary unconsciousness, with a shout which was audible to other people in the room, but not to Gilbey himself, who did not know at the time what had happened.

No less remarkable are the accounts given by the doyen of

* Author of *Secret Fighting Arts of the World*, also published by Pan.

British students of the martial arts, E. J. Harrison himself, author of numerous books on jiu-jitsu, judo and karate, including the authoritative *The Fighting Spirit of Japan*, and certainly for long the best-informed westerner on both the theory and practice of at least the Japanese martial arts. Harrison explains that he has not himself witnessed some of the more startling demonstrations of this technique, such as the power to cause birds to fall from trees, apparently lifeless, and restore them to full activity again, by use of the *kiai*. However, he did have two personal experiences of the occult powers of a veteran of the martial arts, Mr Nobuyuki Kunishige. The first at least seems to have involved nothing that could not be regarded as hypnotism. Mr Kunishige seems to have persuaded a young boy dying in terrible pain that the two of them were going to visit a firework festival. The child instantly responded to what was presumably an hypnotic spell, and died painlessly and happy, convinced that he was actually at the festival. The other incident duplicates Gilbey's story. A young girl was suffering from chronic and violent nose-bleeds. Local doctors were totally unable to control the attacks. Mr Kunishige permanently stopped the bleeding first from one nostril, then from the other, with two *kiais*, uttered with an intervening lapse of some days. Harrison also reports that doctors in the district testified to Kunishige's power to revive people who had been given up for dead, so that they could be cured by orthodox medicine.[2]

It is impossible not to find this confusing. Harrison, as we shall see, is generally ready to concede that the explanation of this and other extraordinary displays might lie in hypnotism. However, some of Kunishige's feats cannot possibly be regarded as deriving from any use of hypnotism as we understand it, simply because he appears to have been able to work on unconscious or unwilling minds, to affect bodily processes in no way related to the voluntary muscles. Nose-bleeds are not a matter for the will. Moreover, both Harrison and Kunishige also consider the effects described to be produced in some way by the *kiai*. This has two more difficulties. In the first place, they cannot be produced by hypnotism if they are produced by the *kiai*, so one really has to make a choice. In the second place, it is none too easy to see how the physiological explanation given for the working of the *kiai* really applies in the examples given.

The physiological explanation usually offered is that the *kiai*-shout produces sound-waves or vibrations which have the power to affect the desired parts of the human body in the desired way. The favourite illustration is that of the violin or the operatic tenor breaking wine glasses or even windows with particular notes sustained at the appropriate pitch for the appropriate time. This is made the more convincing when one considers other examples of occult phenomena of this kind. The Japanese are by no means the only people who claim to be able to produce sound waves in a manner decidedly out of the ordinary. W. Y. Evans-Wentz in his book *Tibet's Great Yogi Milrepa* (OUP)[3] refers to the belief of the Tibetans that certain occult phrases or *mantras* have the power to disintegrate objects of which they happen to be the key-note or with which they are in vibratory accord. This is not quite the same thing as the simple impact of waves upon a fragile surface, of course. No less extraordinary a use of sound waves is reported by Dr Alfonso Caycedo in his book *India of Yogis* (National Publishing House, Delhi, 1966) where he describes the ability of Swami Nada Bramananda to cause his voice to move in any direction, thus producing vibrations 'at the crown of his head, navel or hands', or 'along any limb to any part of the anatomy like electricity', or even along the base of his spinal column. More significantly still, the Swami could apparently use his powers of voice-direction to make the tendons in the back of his hand vibrate in time, with a force which could not be checked by four men holding his arm.[4] This latter exploit certainly matches the performance of Koichi Tohei's upraised little finger, described later in this chapter, although again we seem to be faced with a different kind of power, used in a different way.

The trouble with any physiological explanation of kiai-jutsu

and comparable vibratory techniques is indeed that the vibrations concerned may seem to have normal physical origins
from the vocal chords and the roof of the mouth, but they are
certainly subject to mental direction in a way which is not
explicable in normal physical terms. We have undoubtedly
moved from the area of anatomy to that of the occult. Worse
still, these vibrations can apparently be made to operate in a
way totally unlike that of normal sound waves. Sound waves
can indeed smash glasses and break windows and also drive
people crazy. But they do not seem to be physically capable of
doing anything else. The masters of kiai-jutsu on the other
hand seem to be able to do almost anything they like with their
sound waves. They can stop nosebleeds, restore the injured to
mobility and the unconscious to their senses, and check John
F. Gilbey at the moment of onslaught, without his being
aware of it, and without any similar effect on other people
in the room. Even if one could imagine sound waves doing
all this in some way, one would still be faced with the problem
of how the mechanism of the human body could be operated
with the incredible subtlety required to produce waves
which would have just precisely the effect desired, and no
other.

Harrison naturally makes the obviously logical next step, and
suggests that any occult effects are in fact more likely to be
produced by some force transmitted through the *kiai*, rather
than by the *kiai* itself. The *kiai* thus becomes merely another
channel for intrinsic energy. Such a force could obviously be
transmitted just as effectively through some other medium. On
the other hand, it is equally possible that the bodily exercises
performed by the masters of kiai-jutsu might well help one to
acquire intrinsic energy, even if this was not their ostensible
purpose. The fact is indeed that the exercises are in all respects
essentially the same as those recommended by every other
occult school of combat or physical training. There is no mystery about them. The kiai-jutsu masters were not concerned to
keep any secrets. The student is recommended succinctly and
precisely to:

stand or be seated upright and face the rising sun ... Keep your eyes partly open while breathing, which latter must be deep and calm. Close your teeth and exhale slowly through the mouth ... as the fresh morning breeze expels mist. Inhale quietly from the nostrils and refresh your blood by filling your *tanden* [abdomen] with air invigorated by the sun's rays ... draw in the air little by little until your *tanden* is full. In doing so endeavour to swell the latter, assisting this operation with your hands. Remain in this condition until you can no longer bear it ... keep your body soft, hold your shoulders well drawn down, your back bent forward, and sit in such a manner that the tip of your nose hangs over your *saika tanden* [navel]. Accustom yourself when sitting to press the seat with your hips, as it were, and when walking to project your abdomen beyond your feet.

One hardly knows whether to describe this posture as being relaxed or tense. It is at least certainly receptive and not easily distracted. Its purpose is indeed to encourage something like total detachment of mind, so that whatever is happening to one physically will not be impeded by irrelevant mental activity. This can further be guarded against by use of

Munen mushin – that is, the name of Buddha. When you open your mouth wide to expel the air you get *na* and when you shut your mouth to inhale the air you get *mu*. When next you open your mouth you get *a*, and when again you close it you get *mi*. When again you open your mouth you get *da*, and when again you shut it you get *butsu*. Thus the thrice repeated exhalation and inhalation is equivalent to the Buddhist invocation 'Namu Amida Butsu', which is symbolical of the letters *a* and *um*. The sound *a* is produced by opening the mouth and the sound *um* by shutting it. It may therefore be said that in the state of total absence of mind [*munen mushin*] you are always repeating the name of Buddha, even if you do not pronounce it aloud.

We started with the idea that anybody who really knew what he was doing could probably hit as hard without the *kiai*-shout as with it. Where this argument has led is to the apparently contrary idea that anybody who really worked on the *kiai* would thereby acquire powers which would enable him almost to dispense with crude physical strength. This at least was the line of thought which presented itself early to the man who unquestionably merits the title of the greatest karateka of them all, Masutatsu Oyama, a Korean of herculean muscularity, appalling aspect and incredible athletic skill.

Oyama experimented with two of his students. One was trained on calisthenics and hand-hardening techniques, while the other concentrated on meditation and breathing exercises, without attempting to harden his body in any specific ways. It was discovered after six months that the second student had not only developed a superior karate technique to the first, but could also break almost as many bricks as his rival, despite the fact that he had done nothing to toughen the surface of his knuckles, while the other had ornamented his with impressively insensitive callouses.[5]

Nor could some karateka merely deliver punishment in a way which did not seem to be wholly explicable physically. Some found that they could resist blows with hardwood staves on their extended forearms. It was admittedly not unusual for a karateka to toughen the outer edge of his arm, but nobody ever toughened the inner edge, which was where the blows actually landed. It was true that the subjects in these experiments employed maximum physical tension in their arms, in an attempt to 'focus' strength, but it was not clear that this would really help them much: tensed muscles can certainly cushion a blow, but they also feel it intensely. Moreover, adepts in Laotian karate went a stage further: a karateka would lie down on a bench; a number of bricks would be placed on his bare back; and an assistant would then smash the bricks with a steel bar, without damaging the man underneath.

To make an obvious point, something out of the ordinary was going on here. Any protective muscularity is extremely sparse on the back, and can in any case be tensed only by an unusual feat of muscle control. The back is also the last place where one could easily develop callouses. But even more convincing evidence was soon available, that the oriental martial artists were at their most developed calling upon forces which did not seem to belong to the physical universe, properly so-called.

The Japanese karateka had of course long been aware of the existence on the Asian mainland of a style of fighting known vaguely as 'Chinese boxing'. Serious studies of karate almost invariably contained maps showing how pugilistic techniques had spread from China to Korea, and thence to Okinawa and Japan, while another cultural movement carried the arts through South-East Asia as far as Indonesia. The trouble was that nobody outside of China seemed at all sure what it was that the Chinese themselves actually did, and how far the Chinese forms of the martial arts had been altered during their diffusion over the rest of Asia. One thing that did seem clear was that the specifically Chinese styles did differ very much indeed from any of the known forms of karate. What was also undeniable was that the Chinese pugilists themselves invariably expressed the greatest possible contempt for karate, and indeed for all the other martial arts as well, except for Indian boxing, which they honoured as a revered ancestor, and of which even less if possible was known than of Chinese boxing; that they treated the other Asian arts as mere corruptions of the true Chinese art of self-defence; and that they seemed to have uncomfortably sound reasons for adopting these disagreeable attitudes. Japanese and western boxers alike were repeatedly humiliated whenever they managed to take part in contests with exponents of the apparently innumerable varieties of Chinese boxing. Chinese masters showed their ability to perform any and all of the plank-breaking and tile-shattering stunts of the karateka without any of the customary yells, contortions, muscular effort, and particularly without the protection of the swollen and calloused knuckles of the karateka; and karateka competing in the semi-official martial arts contests in Taiwan, in which bouts were fought to a finish and nothing was barred save blows to eye or groin, invariably finished last, with the Chinese artists just as invariably winning.

This was clearly the stage at which in Oyama's own words, the martial arts 'approached the portals of the supernatural'.[6]

His honesty in recognizing this has of course earned him ever since the condemnation of sceptics, especially of those generally self-appointed karate *senseis*, mainly outside Japan, dedicated to the profession of training muggers for profit. It was obvious that the mugger-trainers and sceptics had a valid point: there was no doubt that one could learn a great deal about self-defence, as well as about assault and battery, without any acquaintance with the occult or anything remotely bearing on culture. One would naturally be totally destroying a great tradition by doing so, but that was not likely to bother the people concerned. There was also the fact that Oyama was knocking the foundations from under classical karate himself: the Chinese techniques which he was praising as superior to those of orthodox karate also happened to differ in almost every possible way from those of karate. The karateka kept his spine erect; the Chinese boxer deliberately rounded his shoulders and compressed his chest. The karateka hit with a horizontal fist; the Chinese boxer with a vertical one. The karateka yelled; the Chinese usually kept quiet, or at most snorted. The karateka hit straight forward; the Chinese allegedly preferred to hit and block with a circular motion. The karateka hit with the hand furthest from his opponent; the Chinese with either, but preferably with the one nearest. The karateka used one hand at a time; the Chinese preferably used both. The karateka blocked and hit separately; the Chinese simultaneously. If one system was right, the other hardly could be.

That being the case, it is difficult to see why Oyama has continued to teach what is recognizably a form of classical karate, admittedly made far more eclectic and flexible. Bewildered British critics indeed suggest that what Oyama is now teaching as 'advanced' karate appears to be not karate at all, but a form of jiu-jitsu. The fact is that orthodox karate is now vanishing. It has indeed suffered the same fate as western boxing, by being taught for commercial motives as a kind of sport, rather than as a system of self-defence. The emphasis on tournament-winning techniques has corrupted classical methods into a *mélange* of mauling, hauling, showmanship and fakery without system or logic, let alone without spiritual pretensions of any kind. Even this degeneration has not saved karate as a spectator sport, any more than corruption preserved jiu-jitsu. It is now being challenged by the least occult and perhaps least sophisticated of all forms of combat, Thai kick-boxing, a species of incompetent savate, devoid of all the techniques which make for effective fighting with either hands or feet. As Robert W. Smith succinctly informs us, the Thai boxers seem unaware of the discovery of either the straight left or the uppercut; they jab with the leading foot, a singularly unprofitable manoeuvre; and they use the back foot essentially in a kind of hook kick, which must certainly be the easiest of all blows to evade or parry. The limitations of this oriental misfortune were convincingly shown when French middleweight savate champion Guillaume recently won all five of his contests against Asian kick-boxers by knock-outs, three in the first round, using the most basic of all savate techniques. He would lead with a straight left to the jaw, then kick his opponent in the stomach. End of contest.

Shorinji kempo

But the final blow to orthodox karate has undoubtedly come from Japan itself, where the self-defence forces are now being taught a system of unarmed combat, based not on judo or karate as in the past, but on the austerely occult and fundamentally Chinese art of shorinji kempo: Kempo has admittedly been condemned by Robert W. Smith as being merely 'a Japanized form of Chinese boxing', unlike anything he ever saw in China. It therefore calls for little description here, as its techniques and principles are essentially those of the internal school of Chinese boxing, considered more fully in the next section. It is sufficient to say at this point that shorinji kempo uses vertical fist blows, prefers short jabbing punches, blocks with the minimum of effort and places tremendous emphasis on meditation in order to generate what is called vaguely 'spiritual force'.

There is no doubt as to what this force is supposed to be able to do. The shorinji masters claim that the use of spiritual force enables one to kill with even the lightest of blows. This is admittedly an art which it is hard to demonstrate convincingly in public. The shorinji masters were in any case admirably reluctant to publicize just how these powers might be obtained. In this they were only following the example of their Chinese teachers, who were the people most reluctant of any on earth to let foreigners have the benefits of any profitable discoveries which they might have made themselves. But their chances of keeping their occult arts secret vanished with the 1940s. Even before karate itself had begun to decline, a whole team of Japanese martial artists were coming forward, fully prepared to demonstrate and explain to anybody who cared to come along, techniques fully as incredible as those hinted at by the shorinji kempo masters. What was more, these Japanese stylists claimed to have incorporated their occult techniques into a system of self-defence which even in material terms was one of the most rational, as well as undoubtedly the safest, of all the combat arts of the world. There has never been anything quite like aikido.

3 The unbendable arm:
aikido

Aikido first impinged upon the western consciousness in 1951 when Minoru Mochizuki from Aikikai Headquarters in Tokyo introduced the art to France. Two years later, Koichi Tohei, present head of the Instruction Department of the Tokyo Aikikai, demonstrated aikido techniques in San José. This was a considerably more spectacular performance, which did not go unrecorded. Tohei successfully and easily threw five large and experienced American judo competitors who attacked him simultaneously. This led to the most extraordinary phenomenon in the history of the martial arts. It was not just that aikido became popular. It has indeed remained an art for the comparative few. Its popularity still nowhere near approaches that of karate or judo: latest figures indicate that there are about 6,500 practitioners of aikido in the United States, compared with 29,500 judoka and 120,000 karateka. What is really remarkable about aikido is simply that for the first time in the West a martial art based unambiguously upon the use of occult powers was offered seriously to the general public, and the offer was taken seriously.

There is no need to equivocate about this. The pretensions of the aikidoists are literally fantastic. So is their success in getting these pretensions accepted at something like their face value. Tohei Sensei's feats in San José did not of course necessarily mean more than that he was rather better than the judoka at their own game. His task could even be said to have been made simpler by the fact that he was attacked by five men at the same time, because they would obviously get in their own way. It is in any case easier to defend oneself with judo than it is to attack. But the powers to which Tohei himself attributed his success in his book *Aikido* were of an order quite different from any publicly claimed by any judoka, or indeed any other exponent of the Asian martial arts until then. Tohei illustrated his book with pictures of himself demonstrating among other things the use of what he called the 'unbendable arm' technique. These photographs seemed to show on the one hand that without any exertion of muscular strength Tohei could resist the attempts of a man far bigger and more muscular than himself to bend his relaxed, partially extended arm; and on the other hand, that, equally without discernible effort on his part, he could render his mammoth partner helpless with a wrist-lock applied with one hand.

It was not hard to see how the wrist-lock could be made to work in practice. The unbendable arm seemed simply inexplicable in terms of any imaginable physical response on Tohei's part. But this was only the beginning. Tohei's book was followed by a brilliantly comprehensive paperback by the American orientalist Jay Gluck, in which Gluck described how he had seen Tohei resist the attempts of three vast members of 545 Military Police Company of the United States Army to push him over, even though Tohei was holding them off only with the tip of his little finger, which Gluck insisted was always vertical. Tohei was not even poking the policemen with his extended finger, not that it would presumably have made much difference if he had. Indeed, not only were these three huge American policemen unable to push Tohei back against the power extruded from his little finger, they were indeed forced rapidly to move backwards themselves 'at a flick of his upraised pinky', as Mr Gluck puts it.

Nor was even this all. Mr Gluck went on to describe how the doyen of aikido, Morihei Uyeshiba, some four foot ten inches in height, eighty-five years old at the time, and probably not much more than six stone in weight, evaded all attempts to seize him made by no less than five United States Military Policemen, this time from 825 Company, backed up by half a dozen Japanese judo and karate black belt holders, and Japanese swordsmen armed with oak swords. It must have been quite a shambles. Mr Gluck also reported that Uyeshiba could barehandedly fend off arrows fired at him pointblank; that he could similarly avoid even pistol bullets fired pointblank at him by a marksman; and that he was able to disarm a man carrying a pistol from fifty yards away. The younger Koichi Tohei could repeatedly disarm Frank Goody, judoka, ex-Marine hand-to-hand combat instructor and police marksman from eighteen feet. He could also successfully resist the efforts of two Military Policemen to tip him off an unstable four-legged stool, only three of whose legs could touch the ground at the same time, even though Tohei himself was sitting on the stool with both feet raised off the floor, so that he could offer no opposing leverage at all.

People who are being asked to believe the physically impossible have a right to ask what is going on. Here the inevitable confusion arose at once. A few judoka, moved to indignation by the reports of what Tohei's upraised pinky had been able to achieve in San José and Tokyo, pointed out the obvious truths that Tohei was a man of tremendous muscular capacity, indeed built like a tank, as well as being notably stocky, with a centre of gravity near to the ground even by Japanese standards. He might thus very well be able to defeat the efforts of a normal man to bend or unbend his arm by simple brute force. If it was objected that Tohei was in fact resisting the efforts of men far bigger and by any test stronger than himself, without apparently exerting any physical force himself at all, it was replied that Tohei's elbow joint was 'pointing at a diagonal out and down', so that 'his whole body was displaced sideways', thereby making it peculiarly hard to get adequate leverage against him. Another suggestion was that Tohei was applying some kind of counter-leverage, like that supposed to have been used by former world bantamweight boxing champion Johnny Coulon, who at the age of sixty-seven toured the world, defying anybody to lift him off a platform.

All these objections had the same practical difficulties. In the first place, the scientists who explained Tohei's and Coulon's ability to resist pressure in terms of leverage were not themselves able to duplicate what should have been the simplest physical trick. In the second place, Tohei at least was clearly not applying any counter-force to the people trying to shift him. Thirdly, even if Tohei was using some kind of body displacement to perform his unbendable arm stunt, he could not have been using body displacement or any other kind of physical force to perform his more remarkable feats. There are limits to what even the strongest of men can do with his upraised but untensed pinky. And finally, there was the simple psychological fact that nobody who had any acquaintance with Tohei Sensei or any of the other leading aikidoists could imagine them as charlatans. No one could reasonably doubt that they believed they could do what they seemed to be able to do, and they believed that they were doing it through the instrumentality of occult powers.

The aikidoists themselves made no secret of the origin of their powers. Aikido remains by far the most open of the occult arts. It has two bases, one physical and one metaphysical. The first is simply circular movement. This is not entirely new. Most of the more practical jiu-jitsu techniques also use it, as we have seen. But the more complicated and less practical ones do not, and in no sense could one describe circular motion as the basis of jiu-jitsu, as it is of aikido. It is simply one of the methods that jiu-jitsu employs, along with pushing, pulling, tripping, sacrifice throws, strangling, kicking, punching and presumably biting, as the opportunity arises. The jiu-jitsuian has a truly comprehensive armoury. His real problems are to remember which particular weapon he should employ, and why that particular one.

This is almost equally true of the judoka, whose commitment to tripping and throwing his opponent gives him a perhaps more automatic response than the jiu-jitsu exponent, but who in general has even more varied and complicated moves to perform to achieve his desired end. It is less true of the karateka who has his stylized response to most self-defence situations of get-set, block, punch, get-set, punch. But this has its own problems and dangers. By contrast, the aikidoist has a standard,

logical, instantaneous, promising and safe response, adaptable
to almost any conceivable situation. In contrast to the jiu-jitsuian, he will almost always move in the same way at the beginning, so there is no question of his having to think what to
do; in contrast to the judoka, he has not got both hands tied up
while his opponent is still free to kick and clobber him; and in
contrast to the karateka, he is using both hands simultaneously,
and is covered at every stage of his response.

This is where circular movement comes in. It means in essence that the defender turns his arms and body to follow the
direction of an attack, thus in essence diverting it past him,
instead of meeting it head on with opposing force as the karateka almost invariably does. This necessarily upsets the balance
of the attacker forward. The aikidoist will then swing back in
the opposite direction, so that he has completed an 'S-turn',
using the attempts of the assailant to recover his balance, to flip
him backwards. In practical terms, this means that the aikidoist
under attack simply hits his opponent in the face or ribs, turns,
seizes his wrist, pushes his elbow and flips him over. There are
really not all that many situations in which this response does
not at least have a chance of working. It is indeed about as
foolproof as any practical method can be. If your opponent fails
to parry the initial blow to the face, it will probably disconcert
him sufficiently for you to grab the wrist of the attacking arm,
and get on with the job of twisting him off-balance. If he does
parry it, then you can grab the wrist of the parrying arm, and
start on that. If you can neither disconcert him nor twist him,
you have the consolation that no other technique would have
been likely to work either.

Aikido action thus neither wastes time, nor restricts the
range of response. It is immediate, and it offers endless variety.
It is also clearly not very mysterious so far. But there is mystery. Part of the mystery is as usual caused by the consciously
or unconsciously misleading statements of the people who write
about aikido. We have already seen Jay Gluck's account of
aikidoists disarming gunmen from distances of from eighteen
to fifty feet. But in fact the real disarming would have to be

done from a distance of not more than three feet, at most. It is
also unlikely that Frank Goody was really trying to shoot
Tohei. It should not be too difficult to dodge any marksman
who is not trying to hit you, especially if you know in advance
when he is going to shoot. More serious are statements like
Gluck's that aikido 'unlike karate and kempo ... includes no
blows. Unlike judo it really includes no grips or throws.' Even
Morihei Uyeshiba claims that 'there is no form and no style in
aikido'. However, the fact is that aikido, far from having no
blows, almost always uses a blow as its first response to any
kind of attack. Nor are the blows indiscriminate as they tend to
be in jiu-jitsu. There is a precise allotment of foreknuckle-fist
to the ribs, back-fist to the bridge of the nose, and knife-hand to
face or rib cage. So there are blows. Morihei Uyeshiba indeed
warns specifically that 'a single blow in aikido can kill', though
undoubtedly in aikido one kills only with the best intentions
and without malice. There are also grips. Stage two of the
aikido response involves a wrist-lock, which in turn leads to an
arm-pin, which, as was convincingly demonstrated to the present author, is so far from being merely a punishing hold, that it
can in fact break the victim's arm in three places. Nor is there
any question that every aikido contest ends with one of the
parties having been propelled off-balance and conveyed un-
willingly to the floor, normally through the air, which constitutes a 'throw' in any sense of the term.

It is equally true that aikido has a characteristic and
invariable fighting stance, as will be discussed later, and an
equally characteristic manner of walking and turning, which
again is what is normally meant by 'form and style', even if it
does not have a set sequence of shadow-boxing routines, as in a
karate or shao-lin 'form'. But one of the things that helps to
make the occult side of the oriental fighting arts so baffling is of
course that words are normally not used in their 'normal' sense.
For example, the term 'circular movement', which seems clear
enough, and can in fact be related to most aikido defences without difficulty, has to be qualified, as Dr Robert W. Smith has
explained, with the reservation that the Chinese and Japanese

frequently describe as circular motions which any other people would describe as straight. Hence one repeatedly finds that combat systems which their exponents claim are always circular, in fact contain blatantly straightforward movements. An aikidoist will thus normally go inside any long movement by an attacker with a straight left to the jaw. The explanation given is that the Chinese and Japanese regard a circle as being made up of innumerable straight lines. Any straightforward movement is thus really part of a circle whose circumference is infinity. It makes sense, but it is perhaps not something which an untutored westerner could very well be expected to work out for himself.

There is a lot more about aikido that he could hardly work out for himself. There seems at first little to understand. The physical base of aikido is not mysterious at all. It could be described without much distortion as a supremely economical and systematized form of jiu-jitsu. But this is only the beginning. The real and extremely mysterious element of aikido lies in the second of its bases, the metaphysical base, symbolized by Tohei's vertical pinky.

Aikido had its true origin in a supernatural revelation. It had its historical precursors of course in the first attempts to devise systems of hand-to-hand fighting in Japan, known as 'daito aikijutsu', supposedly founded by Prince Teijun, the sixth son of the Emperor Seiwa, between AD 850 and 880. It was handed down through members of the Minamoto family, and became known after 1574 as the Aizutodome technique, after the name of the town to which the then head of the family had moved. In 1868 his successor, Sokaku Takeda sensei, began to teach the art outside his family. Takeda met Morihei Uyeshiba in 1911. Uyeshiba was then twenty-eight, five foot two inches in height, 180 pounds in weight, and not surprisingly three or four times as strong as most other men. This human tank understandably impressed Takeda as an exceptionally promising pupil.

Uyeshiba, however, left Takeda in 1918, when his father became seriously ill. He then attached himself to the Revd Wanisaburo Deguchi, founder of a new religion based on human love and goodness as a means to world unity. Uyeshiba attempted after his father's death to find ultimate truth beyond the practice of the martial arts. His disciples record that during this period he developed the art of anticipating an opponent's intention. Thus he was able to disarm a bandit in Mongolia who held him up at pistol-point, because he became aware of the gunman's intention to shoot him before he was actually able to pull the trigger. In 1925, a Japanese naval officer attacked him with an oak sword, but was similarly unable to hit because Uyeshiba always knew where the officer was going to strike before he actually did so, and simply moved somewhere else. He then, as he records, went for a walk in the garden to cool down. While doing so, he found himself rooted immovably to the ground; the universe quaked; and a golden light came up from the ground and changed Uyeshiba's body into a golden one. Uyeshiba then became aware of the mind of God, which explained to him that the true source of the martial arts is Divine love.

This was the point at which the new art of aikido developed from the existing arts of jiu-jitsu. Uyeshiba interpreted his experience, whatever it might have been, to mean that all the universe was one, and that the true aim of the martial arts must therefore be to be in harmony with the universe. This would mean that 'when an enemy tries to fight with me, the universe itself, he has to break the harmony of the universe. Hence at the moment he has the mind to fight with me, he is already defeated.' Hence of course the principle of turning movement. By turning with an opponent's attack, one does not oppose his movement, although one certainly opposes what he is trying to do. One moves in harmony with his movement. Both are therefore in harmony with the universe. And because one is in harmony with the universe, one can serve as a channel through which the force of the universe can move, thereby drawing on one's opponent with all the force of creation, or at least as much of it as can move through one's own body at the time.

This is what the whole concept of mind over matter is all about. Whatever terms are used, it comes back to the idea of an external power which is not subject to the laws of the physical universe, but can be introduced into them by a certain kind of mental disposition. Hence Uyeshiba's formation of the word aikido, from the Japanese *ai* meaning 'love' or 'harmony'; *ki* (Chinese *ch'i*) meaning at the simplest 'spirit'; and *do* meaning 'way of'. Hence we have either 'the way of the harmonious spirit' or perhaps 'the way of spiritual harmony'. Whatever we have, we have at least the notion that a certain mental attitude, leading to a certain arrangement of the body, allows one to employ the actual creative force which gives origin to the physical universe. One is using 'soul power' in the literal sense of the words. It might of course be truer to the concept to say that one is being used by the creative force, in that one is simply allowing it to flow into the physical universe through oneself, by moving in harmony with it.

This of course raises the basic question of whether there is such a thing as a creative or intrinsic force, which practitioners of aikido are able to utilize, whether they are putting it at their, or themselves at its service. The first objection is naturally that there is again nothing out of the ordinary happening there at all. This, as has been seen, is extraordinarily difficult to sustain. Critics can certainly point to a number of lamentable public exhibitions where performers, usually karateka rather than aikidoists, have either failed in their efforts to produce any evidence of *ki* in action, or at least have done nothing which could not be accounted for adequately by simple muscular effort. But this kind of negative argument is not enough. It is unquestionably difficult to prove the existence of occult forces, but it can be almost as difficult to disprove it. All the failures or frauds in the world cannot invalidate one successful and non-fraudulent display. The fact is that sooner or later the critic has to be prepared to denounce someone as a liar. This is particularly inescapable in the case of aikido. We are not dealing here with something that can be dismissed as merely mistaken belief. One does not normally feel required to call a Roman Catholic priest a liar if he claims to be able to turn bread and wine into flesh and blood in the performance of a ritual which

one does not believe in oneself. There is no question of fakery
involved, because there is no attempt to provide physical evidence that he has done what he claims to have done. One either
believes or one does not. But the masters of aikido do claim to
provide physical evidence of their possession of *ki*, and other
people claim to have physical experience of it. The number of
liars involved in deception on this scale becomes quite impressive. One could begin to list old Morihei Uyeshiba, his son Kisshomaru, author of a magnificent book on aikido, Koichi Tohei,
Jay Gluck, the assorted hearties of Companies 545 and 825 of
the United States Military Police, everybody who trained with
any of the above, the present writer, etc.

But it is far more complicated than that. In the first place,
much of the testimony to the powers of Tohei in particular
come from people who are not themselves aikidoists. It is
difficult to imagine that in a field of activity as irradiated with
mutual jealousy as that of the martial arts, so many judoka,
karateka, jiu-jitsuans and kendoists would be prepared to make
their own arts appear ineffective in order to advertise aikido.
The obvious explanation, that Tohei paid them to take falls for
his benefit, has obvious objections. For one thing, as has been
said, nobody sees Tohei Sensei in that kind of role. For another,
there just isn't that much money in aikido to make it worth his
while.

But the most serious objection to a simple dismissal of the
claims of the aikido masters is that their claims are by no means
unique. One of the most convincing reports of personal experience of the kind of power displayed most impressively by
Tohei and the Uyeshibas was from no less than E. J. Harrison
in *The Fighting Spirit of Japan*. In this book, Harrison described how a judo master, Mr Nobuyuki Kunishige, invited
Harrison to pull him by the ears off the cushion on which he
was squatting; how he failed completely to budge the lighter,
older and less muscular Japanese, or even to make him change
expression while dragging hard enough to detach any normal
human ear from a normal human head; and how Kunishige
simply leaned back, and pulled Harrison off balance, still hang-

ing on to his ears. Kunishige then allowed Harrison to apply the full strength of both his hands to the upper joints of the fingers of Kunishige's right hand. Again Harrison applied pressure which by any normal standards should have broken Kunishige's fingers to pieces, and subjected him to quite unbearable pain; again he made not the slightest impression on the Japanese at all; and again Kunishige simply withdrew himself from Harrison's grasp without any apparent effort or any chance of resistance.

Two possible explanations have been offered which do not involve one in the uncomfortable position of denouncing as frauds and liars people who seem on all the evidence to be among the last men on earth to fit into such categories, and who in addition really do not seem to have been able to gain anything from their deceit, assuming that it is such. The first is simply hypnotism. Harrison himself refers to Kunishige's hypnotic powers, and suggests that these and other feats, such as the ability to hold burning tobacco in his fingers without physical effects, might be in some way manifestations of hypnotism. A similar explanation has been offered to discount the arm-wrestling achievements of karate sensei Don Buck of Navato, California. Buck emerges on examination to be one of the most obviously formidable human beings alive, along with Masutatsu Oyama. He was indeed taught by Oyama, having first experimented with Chinese boxing and Zen meditation techniques. His particular art was to win arm wrestling contests in San Francisco. On at least one occasion he won such a contest, using only his little finger. His opponent still claims that he must have been hypnotized. Buck insists that he was not. His explanation is that using one finger put him at an advantage, because he was able to 'focus the same amount of strength into a smaller area'.[1]

It can be said quite simply that nobody would want to call Don Buck a liar. It is also clear that what he is saying is impossible in physical terms. Arm-wrestling is a matter of muscularity, leverage and to a considerably less extent of weight. Not even Don Buck's little finger possesses any of these

qualities in any significant degree. One might as well talk of focusing strength into the little toe of one's left foot. The only
kind of strength which can be focused in such a way is a
strength which is not exercised through any physical equipment, because it is not physical in origin. It has to be intrinsic
force. This might not be the easiest explanation to accept, but it
would be the only one left if we are to exclude hypnotism as a
possibility. The fact that Don Buck has already denied that
hypnotism was used in the case in which he participated, is only
one of the reasons why we are compelled to do so.

This would in any case only be explaining away one aspect of
the occult by attributing its effects to the working of another.
Hypnotism is itself anything but a simple physiological
phenomenon. It is treated as such by the sceptics only because
they are unable seriously to pretend that it does not exist. Dr
G. H. Estabrooks, Professor of Psychology at Colgate University, describes hypnotism as simply a state of exaggerated sug-
gestibility, induced by artificial means. He considers that it is
probably induced in fact by persuading the subject to transfer
to the hypnotist the feelings of submission which he might have
had for his father when he was a child.[2] Dr Estabrooks dis-
misses as 'trash' any notion that the planets might be able to
influence human bodies; pours scorn on Mesmer's original
notions of 'animal magnetism', which read now like a confused
notion of intrinsic energy; and considers that there is nothing
supernatural in the ability of hypnotists to raise blood blisters
on the skins of their subjects by suggestion. However, he also
expresses the view that many aspects of alleged occult phenomena or ESP have not yet been explained; lists numerous cases
where pathological conditions which were in no possible way
mental have been cured by hypnotism; and remarks that it is
possible to influence the autonomic nervous system under hypnotism but not in a waking state, without knowing why this
should be so. This kind of argument really seems to leave too
much unanswered. If in fact the will is capable of producing
physiological effects by order without going through the normal
physiological processes, then there simply must be some other

field in which it operates, and which is not wholly contained within the physical universe. One has to repeat again that things either happen or they do not, and if they happen they must be made to happen in some way. There is indeed not the slightest reason to expect the workings of the will to be anything but mysterious. One of the greatest of living experts on the physiology of the brain, the Australian Sir John Eccles, has publicly claimed that we still understand very little indeed about the way in which our bodies respond to directions from the will, and we know absolutely nothing about why they do. The mechanistic view of man has the great drawback that nobody knows what makes the machine do whatever it is supposed to do.

The hypnotism explanation thus has every possible disadvantage. In the first place, we have no idea why the autonomic system is subject to direction from somebody else's will when one is under hypnosis, and not to one's own will when one is not; there is in any case no way in which to infuse strength through hypnosis into muscles whose fibres did not have that latent power anyway; and finally, we face here the insuperable difficulty that there is no reason to believe that hypnotism was really used in the cases we have looked at. Don Buck denies that he used hypnotism against his opponents; and one cannot see how Harrison could have been hypnotized by Mr Kunishige. Hypnotism demands as a prerequisite that the subject should be put first into a hypnotic trance, from which he emerges without any recollection of what might have been suggested to him during the trance. It is perhaps conceivable that Harrison might have been subjected to such a trance, in which Kunishige suggested to him that he would be unable to pull the latter's ears off or break his finger into fragments, no matter how hard he thought he was trying. However, this seems a pointless and unlikely exercise on Kunishige's part, especially in view of the fact that Kunishige was apparently able to perform feats of kiai-jutsu which cannot possibly be described as due to hypnotic powers, whatever those might be. It seems infinitely more reasonable to suggest that Don Buck, Kunishige and all the other masters are able to exert powers of mind over matter in ways which sometimes resemble the methods of hypnotism, as understood in the West, and sometimes do not. It makes much more sense to argue that hypnotism operates through the *ki*, rather than that the *ki* is an illusion produced by hypnotism. Or one could just say that it is all just a hoax.

We have already seen that the hoax theory involves one in enormous practical difficulties. It is nonetheless rather easier to credit than the various physiological explanations which have been put forward to fit the concept of the *ki* into the framework of the material universe. Jay Gluck, for instance, attempts to apply the theory of hydraulics. He suggests that the technique of the unbendable arm might be explained by attributing to the aikidoist the power to direct the flow of his blood to the limb in question. The arm thus acts like a fire hose, 'limp and easily bent when empty or even when full of still water. But turn on the flow of water and it becomes as rigid as an iron bar.' Gluck illustrates his argument by reference to the fact that 'the male rigidity is a hydraulic action, with blood the fluid'. This is undoubtedly true, and the notion suggests fascinating areas for experiment. It also has an evident applicability here. Gluck draws attention to the fact that many of the basic aikido exercises are clearly designed to stimulate the flow of blood to the arms and fingers. He also observes that photographs of Tohei and Kisshomaru Uyeshiba in particular 'reveal expansions in the arm and leg that seem from their location not to come from muscle but from blood vessels'. Nor is there any doubt that the ability to control the movement of the blood is certainly one of the techniques utilized in the occult martial arts. Thus Serge Martich-Osterman of the Chinese School of Ch'uanfa in Sydney, has demonstrated his ability to drain blood from one part of his body to another to create a cushion to absorb the impact of blows against his vital organs.

John F. Gilbey describes an even more impressive use of what might be described as an opposite technique, by a Japanese master of kiai-jutsu, who could withdraw his blood from the part of his body about to be attacked, so that even cuts with a sword would not be able to make him bleed. This may be associated with the technique known to Chinese boxers for centuries and revealed lately by some karateka, to insulate parts of the body from injury, by 'focusing' strength, whatever that means. Gilbey's teacher, incidentally, mentioned that these methods were not of much practical value in combat, because one does not normally know where one is going to be hit, although they would doubtless have their uses for anybody expecting to be decapitated.

However, this really does not seem to explain satisfactorily what the aikidoists are apparently doing. In the first place, one is faced with the old problem, that the movement of the blood is controlled by the involuntary nervous system, so one still has to explain exactly how the will of the aikidoist exerts control over processes which are not physiologically responsible to it. It is also true that the male organ has the quality of being unbendable only when rigid, if at all, and the unbendable arm of the aikidoist is in fact not rigid, but totally relaxed. The physical states are thus quite dissimilar. It would also appear that Tohei's finger was not rigid during the experiments described, and that it could not possibly have made much difference if it was. Nor presumably were Mr Kunishige's ears rigid when E. J. Harrison was swinging on them. The fact is indeed that the occult force of the *ki* can apparently be used only to transmit power through those parts of the body which are opened to its passage, and it is precisely muscular tension or rigidity which closes the passages for the *ki*.

A certain distinction between aikido and kiai-jutsu clearly emerges here. Confusion naturally arises over the use of terms which are as vague in the original language as in translation. It is of course not surprising to discover that even the masters are unable to define the undefinable, but it does make it difficult to be quite sure what they are talking about. *Ki* for example can mean 'spirit' in the sense of something not limited by time or space; it can also mean 'spirit' in the sense of how a man feels, e.g. 'in good spirit'; it can also, and perhaps most obscurely, mean the original chaos, by the settling of the dust of which the physical universe is supposed to have been created; and finally it has been used to mean 'spirit' in the sense of 'breath'. This last confusing element is the contribution of Kisshomaru Uyeshiba, who persistently refers to *ki* as 'breath power'. But the whole point is that the aikidoist does not expel breath as the karateka is so clearly seen to do. He has no need to, because he is not expending physical energy. He keeps his mouth shut, or smiles gently. It is certainly clear that the karateka or the practitioner of kiai-jutsu must be expelling *ki* through the breath, if we admit that there is anything of the kind to expel, but the aikidoist must be expelling it through his fingertips, if anywhere. *Ki* can undoubtedly be in the breath, but the breath is not the *ki*, any more than the blood is. What the aikidoists claim to be doing is just not explicable in ordinary physical terms.

However, the power to do it can apparently be acquired at least partly by physical means. The aikido masters are quite explicit, if also unfortunately technically vague, about this. First obviously comes the cultivation of a right disposition. One can act as a channel for the force of the universal spirit only if one is oneself in harmony with the universe which is its expression. Morihei Uyeshiba certainly gathered from his experience in the garden that the source of all physical training, in the martial arts in particular, was God's love. One therefore has to banish all thoughts of hatred, rivalry and anything else which might tend to place one in opposition to any part of the universe. One's opponent then in fact is compelled to place himself out of harmony with the universe, and must therefore necessarily be overwhelmed by it.

Cultivating a disposition which is going to be right enough to produce these results might well seem a little difficult. But it is not the way of aikido to try to make things difficult. To put it simply, one could say that position comes before disposition: certain attitudes of the body are appropriate to certain attitudes of mind, and help to bring them on, as it were. The movement of the aikidoists are therefore harmonious above all else, flowing, totally relaxed, and therefore totally and immediately responsive to the needs of any situation. An aikidoist indeed does not ideally react to a situation. He becomes part of the situation. As Zen master Takuan said in his instructions to swordsmen:

Non-interrupting attitude of mind constitutes the most vital element in the art of fencing as well as in Zen. If there is space for even the breath of a hair between two actions, this is interruption. For example, when the hands are clapped, the sound issues without a moment's deliberation ... Likewise one movement must follow another without being interrupted by one's conscious mind.

This mindless, automatic, immediate response makes considerations of speed in the normal sense irrelevant. Thus Kisshomaru Uyeshiba advises his students when countering a straight thrust by the opponent's fist: 'Just think that his reason for thrusting is only to be dodged.'

The stance of the aikidoist must therefore be one perfectly relaxed, perfectly flexible, and adaptable to all situations. He stands in fact with his feet at right angles, as does the western fencer, but with the heel of his front foot in line with the middle of his rear foot, not with its heel. His hands are held open, roughly as if holding an invisible Japanese sword. The body is upright, but the shoulders are lowered, as if held down by heavy weights, and the chest is depressed. There is no tension anywhere. It is perhaps the only fighting stance in the world which is instantly comfortable for the completely untrained man.

One thus is fully informed about the mental disposition and the physical stance most receptive to *ki*. One is also taught swinging graceful movements which give the sensation of irresistible rhythm, which one would presumably feel if the *ki* were in fact flowing, as well as a number of wrist-strengthening exercises which presumably direct the *ki* to one's wrists if it is there to direct, and at least supply them with increased physical power if it is not.

This of course raises one of the most difficult points in the whole consideration of mind over matter. The techniques of

aikido are designed to make one receptive to *ki*, and an appropriate channel for its movement. They are also superbly valuable fighting techniques and excellent physical exercises. A
person trained sufficiently in the bare techniques of aikido,
without any notion of *ki*, will still have a better chance of evad-
ing another person's attack and pinning him with a wrist-lock,
than if he had spent a similar time in practising any other
martial art. But it could be argued that he has not really been
practising aikido, and it certainly could be suggested that they
had been practising a combat art with serious limitations. In
the first place, the aikido masters are quite unequivocal about
the essentially spiritual basis of their art. Uyeshiba himself said
that aikido was not a religion, but was the basis of all religions.
Secondly, many of the defences, such as the use of the arm-pin
against a straight punch, in which one simply turns to allow the
punch to go by, can hardly work at all unless one has something
like telepathic forewarning of the opponent's intention. Even
then the second stage, the capture of the opponent's wrist to
apply the arm-pin, is virtually impossible in normal terms
against someone using short, snapping punches. A defender
unsure of his *ki* is infinitely better advised to try to beat his
opponent to the punch by either punching straight to the jaw
inside the attacking arm, or by kicking to the head over it.
Similarly, the recommended aikido defence against the attacker who grabs your wrist from behind at the same time as he
applies a strangle with his free hand, is to 'swing up your hand-
blades [extended fingers] immediately, move your body to his
left-rear ... be calm and extend power'. This again is a physical impossibility unless one has begun to move before being
attacked, which is hardly to be counted on in the case of the
hold which more than any other is applied as a surprise attack;
or else one is much stronger than one's attacker, which again is
unlikely, as people do not normally attack men obviously
stronger than themselves. The defence will not work without
ki.

This again brings one to the basic question, how does one get
ki? Tohei recommends that one simply believes that one has it.

Ki will flow from one's fingertips if one believes that it is flowing from one's fingertips. But this is only moving the problem a stage further. The whole question of mind over matter necessarily rests on belief, because it rests on will, and the will is ineffective if it is exercised doubtfully or with reservations. But one cannot easily believe to order. Only sheer dogmatism could deny that many aikido exponents have in fact learned to resist and apply force in ways which cannot be explained in terms of either anatomy or physics, as either is normally understood today. They can in other words do the physically impossible at will.

Nor are their abilities confined to combat situations. Tohei Sensei suggests a multitude of ways in which the study of aikido can be beneficial in daily life. For a start, it banishes the fear of death. Since physical dissolution merely allows one to become again part of the true origin of one's being, there is nothing to worry about. In any case, one can expect to live longer in the physical state through the practice of aikido, since the acquisition of a tranquil disposition, in harmony with *ki*, will naturally preserve one from the diseases associated with stress, such as headaches, ulcers and heart failure. It will also render one increasingly invulnerable to one's physical or climatic environment. The successful aikidoist will not be perturbed by extremes of heat or cold. He will cease to be accident-prone, and may also develop surprising capacity to survive those accidents that he does get into. One aikido enthusiast in the United States claimed that he was able to escape intact from an automobile collision because he was able to project a sheltering field of *ki* against the impact. His Volkswagen was wrecked, but he was not.

All this seems too easy. One might indeed argue ungratefully that aikido is too easy. Its rewards seem to be at once so tremendous and so easy to acquire. It is also more than a little vague in both its philosophy and its techniques. One feels that there should be a more precise, more exacting way leading with greater certainty to more concrete and effective results. There is. The way of aikido leads naturally to the way of the ultimate techniques of self-defence and mind over matter, the most precise, most confused, most practical, most fantastic of the occult physical arts, the one now recommended in the United States for everything from levitation to keeping slim, the arts of Chinese boxing.

4 Grand ultimate fists:
Chinese Boxing (tai-chi ch'uan, pa-kua, hsing-i, wing chun, tong long)

Chinese boxing originated in India. This is perhaps the only tolerably dogmatic assertion that one is justified in making at our present stage of knowledge about the supreme achievement of the martial arts. Even this has not passed unchallenged, as indeed one might have expected. Some Black Power apologists have argued that Indo-Aryan culture came originally from Africa, and that the Asian martial arts therefore originated in that continent too. This claim at least can be set aside for the moment as not proven. But so could much else that is claimed about Chinese boxing. What is particularly and infuriatingly obscure is exactly what form of combat it was that the Indians actually introduced to the Chinese.

There is at least no doubt that there was a school of Indian boxing, and that Indians and Chinese pugilists practised together. We have the evidence of historical paintings showing Chinese and Indian boxers working out with each other in gymnasia. Their movements suggest both wide, exaggerated postures of the classical school of Chinese boxing today, as well as the no-nonsense simplicity of the styles which the Chinese actually use in combat. There is also no doubt that cultural movements went from India to China, rather than the other way about, so we can assume safely that it was indeed the Indians who were teaching the Chinese.

What they were teaching them is exactly the problem. The trouble is that even experts in other fields of Indian culture do not know what traditional Indian boxing consisted of, nor in what form it has survived. It is a truly secret art. But it does

exist, despite the general belief of Indian scholars that there are
no separate schools of Indian boxing which can be traced to a
tradition free from and earlier than the European systems.
There is for example a school of the Indian Art of Self-Defence
operating in Penang. Membership is confined to Indians alone,
so one can only guess at what is actually being taught there, but
some of the drills have been photographed for the enlightenment of foreign students of the martial arts. They include basically stick-fighting, the most familiar of all the
Indian modes of combat, in which the staff is held like a bill-
iard cue and used like a long, two-handed sword, unlike the
Japanese style of Bojutsu, where the two hands grasp the staff
at equal distances from the ends. They also include a form of
fist-fighting which seems to resemble Bruce Lee's jeet kune do,
the most austerely simple of all forms of Chinese boxing, in
which nearly all the hitting and most of the parrying is done
with the leading hand, the other being kept close to the body
and used almost solely for warding off or smothering.

This is not much to go on, although it would indicate that at
least one contemporary Indian school uses styles of stick and
fist fighting which resemble those of at least one of the contemporary Chinese schools. But we do in fact have more than
this. There are other Indian schools which observe rituals
steeped in Indian tradition; which employ techniques which
seem to show no trace of western influence whatever, despite
what the Indians themselves might think; and which therefore
might be safely taken as indicating the kind of art which some
Indians must have taught to some Chinese some time ago, and
which alone of the martial arts of the world the Chinese recognize as being as deserving of respect as their own.

Regular bouts of traditional boxing are still carried out twice
a year in India. They are known locally as *mukki,* and take
place only in Benares, as far as is known, in the spring and
autumn festival periods, after harvesting and sowing. The
spring tournaments are held on the day when the Holi festival
is actually observed, i.e. the day when colours are thrown at
passers-by in a carnival mood, immediately after the day on

which the Holi fire is burned. Bouts begin at noon, after the celebrants have stopped throwing colours over one another. They are held in the Brahmaghata, in front of the Rama Mendira, and are followed by ritual bathing. The autumn tournaments follow on 13, 14 and 15 October, at the Durgaghata in Benares, starting at nine or ten o'clock in the evening, and continuing until half past two or three the following morning.

Contestants in both tournaments are grouped into two parties. One consists of the Brahmans, including boxers from the states of Maharastra and Gujerat, together with the best fighters among the local milkmen. It is not exactly obvious why this profession should provide the champions of traditional Indian boxing, unless it be for the same reason that the profession of delivering blocks of ice provided a disproportionate number of fighters in the United States: both occupations impose regular hours, a disciplined way of life, and require continuous muscular effort. There is also of course the fact that traditional Indian boxing, like most of the other Asian martial arts, has emphatic religious associations, and the milkmen are peculiarly honoured in that they work in closer relationship to the cow than anybody else. The other and clearly lesser group of contenders consist of people of the *Sudra varna*, the most inferior of Indian social groups, mostly washermen, and any milkmen who did not qualify for inclusion in the first group. Contenders in each bout are picked on the basis of physique, or on recognition of a challenge made on an earlier occasion.

What happens then is not fully documented, to say the least. Two separate styles are distinguished. In the first, *dhiti mukki*, the arms can be moved freely, presumably in the same way in which a western boxer is free to jab, hook or swing as the occasion presents itself, corresponding to the 'short attack' identified by John F. Gilbey. The second style, the one adjudged superior, is *khadi mukki*, Gilbey's 'long attack', in which the arm is not bent at the elbow but kept perfectly straight like a spear. Blows in *khadi mukki* are delivered by swinging the arms in a circular motion, as in the more formal styles of Chinese boxing. Kicking is regarded as a foul, as well as of dubious utility. Robert W. Smith describes the bouts themselves as probably the roughest form of combat on earth. There is no doubt that displays of bad sportsmanship by a fighter not uncommonly lead to violent brawls among the spectators. Fighters train by hitting bags filled with sand, and by practising the interminable squats and push-ups used by Indian wrestlers.

This is perhaps all that one can affirm with complete certainty. John F. Gilbey indeed provides a considerably more detailed account. In his narrative of his visit to Benares and its environs in 1952, he reports having met two singularly formidable boxers of the traditional Indian school, Dunraj Seth and Srim Baba. The first of these could withstand Gilbey's hardest punch flush in his mouth without the slightest visible effect. He also trained his pupils to develop their fists by hitting with bare knuckles as hard as they could several hours a day against a one-inch thick steel plate, riveted to a concrete wall. Srim Baba was still more impressive. He had acquired through forty-five years' practice an infallible technique of striking at an opponent's testicles; he could without effort and without previous experience perform the three hardest gymnastic exercises in the world at least as well as Gilbey himself could; and even more remarkable, he could strike the top brick of a pile of five, transmitting power through the first and second bricks, which were left intact, and pulverizing the third, without damaging the fourth and fifth.

These arts unfortunately do not seem to have been publicly demonstrated. Gilbey himself does not supply photographs of what he claims to have witnessed, although he did draw pictures of Srim Baba striking for the testicles with a vertical fist. The whole episode would seem totally incredible, at least for anyone still inclined to regard the physically impossible as incredible. But as so often happens, Gilbey has recently received something like corroboration. At the very least, somebody else has come forward with the same story, and this time with photographs. The Malaysian correspondent of the authoritative martial arts magazine *Black Belt*, Teoh Hood Eng, reported in the February 1972 issue of the periodical, that kung-fu exponent Kah Wah Lee has rediscovered the art of the vibrating palm, with which he can duplicate Srim Baba's feat, as well as another incomprehensible technique narrated by Gilbey, the 'delayed death touch'. Lee placed two pieces of half-inch-thick roofing tile under two boards, having sandwiched between them a cushion of soft bean curd of custard-like consistency, about three inches thick. He applied his right palm to the board on top. What happened then is a little more difficult to describe exactly. Lee says that he converted his *ch'i* (intrinsic energy) by intense concentration into resonating vibrations. These were transmitted through the bean curd to the lower board and thence to the tiles, which were shattered by the resonance. The delayed death touch is supposed to work similarly. One applies the vibrating palm to the chest of the victim. The vibrations then enter the body and disrupt the blood flow and lung structure, at a rate determined by the time at which the assailant wants his victim to die.[1]

One can only say again that these things either happened as they have been described, or they did not. People who give every impression of being honest and serious-minded say that they did happen. The only thing that can be affirmed without hesitation is that physical explanations are no more appropriate here than they are with aikido or kiai-jutsu. There is no physical apparatus in the body that can produce vibrations of the required speed and subtlety; there is no conceivable means by which one can control the force or distance of vibrations transmitted through solid objects so that they will cause damage only at a designated point; and there is certainly no physical way in which one can modify the rate of the disruptive impact of vibrations, so that they will kill a person on schedule a day, a week, a year or ten years after he has been subjected to them. The mystery here is increased by the fact that one can again find two different analogies for the process apparently being described. In the first place, the technique of mobilizing the *ch'i* to produce vibrations presumably corresponds to the ability of Swami Nada Bramananda to direct vibrations to any part of his body, cause them to fluctuate in a desired rhythm, and intensify them so vigorously that they cannot be suppressed by the strength of several men. The objective is naturally different, but the same process must surely be involved. Secondly, one must note that this is not the only means by which the Asians claim to be able to produce the effect of delayed death. The austerely high-principled masters of shorinji kempo claim that electricity, which in this case can be equated with intrinsic energy, travels along fourteen routes throughout the human body. Along these fourteen routes there are 708 'holes' or 'switches'. These correspond to the openings used in acupuncture, which we shall be dealing with later. Pressure on any one of these 'holes' either stimulates the intrinsic energy within the body, producing desirable consequences, or else interrupts its movement or short-circuits it in some way, producing paralysis, illness or death. Shorinji kempo teaches that an expert can touch one of these holes in such a way that the effects for good or ill will not manifest themselves for two or three days, thus giving him time to get out of the district and acquire an alibi before his victim starts to fall apart.

This is clearly not quite the same technique as that of the vibrating palm. However, it produces the same results in the same kind of way. It is also just as incredible and unreasonable. It is quite impossible to imagine a person's being able to touch a minute spot on somebody else's body with such delicacy as to be able to ensure that the person so touched will either get better in some specific way, become ill or die, just as desired, and just when desired. It is exactly the same kind of logical problem that one has with kiai-jutsu: the same means, according to the will of the person employing it. There is no reason why the results should be different, except that the master wants them to be. One is again forced to the conclusion that perhaps the technique does not really matter very much. What matters is the will of the person using it. We are in a world where things happen not because there is any physical reason why they should happen, but because somebody has decided that he wants them to happen.

Perhaps they do not happen at all. In that case we have collected a few more names to add to the sceptic's interminable list of dupes and liars of assorted creeds, races, times, places and cultures. However, if by any chance Eng, Lee, Gilbey, Dr Caycedo, Swami Nada Bramananda and the shorinji kempo pontiffs are any of them telling the truth, they have certainly made a contribution to historical scholarship as well as to human understanding of the occult: they have discovered a technique which clearly links the Chinese and traditional Indian schools of boxing. This would seem to be the only one. The great problem in this field of study has hitherto been that even experts in other aspects of Indian culture seem to have no detailed knowledge at all of the methods of what must have been the oldest and may have been the most sophisticated of all the occult combat arts of the East. This lack of information has of course made it impossible to know exactly what connection traditional Indian boxing really had with the development of the Chinese styles. Until someone can tell us what the Indians did, we cannot have much idea what effect it had on what the Chinese do. For the time being, one can only conclude that it might well have had very little effect at all.

This admittedly was not the way things looked a few years ago. Currently available books on Chinese boxing still faithfully report that the art was introduced into China by the Buddhist monk Bodhidharma, who travelled from India to northern China, at a time of great spiritual awakening in India, and took residence in the Shao-lin monastery (Sil-Lum) during the Liang dynasty (AD 506–556). The story then normally continues that Bodhidharma was concerned to observe that some of the novices at the monastery were in too poor physical shape to perform their spiritual exercises properly, or even to stay awake during his lectures. Bodhidharma accordingly devised a set of exercises for them, which eventually developed into a system of unarmed combat, from which the other schools of Chinese boxing derived over the centuries.

This at least gave a tidy pattern of origin and development to what would otherwise have been the untidiest of all fields of study. Unfortunately, there seems not the slightest reason to believe any of it. The exercises which Bodhidharma is supposed to have developed are listed in the *I Chin Ching*, which he is supposed to have written, and which is most easily comprehensible as a book on fortune telling. However, it is now agreed by scholars that all known versions of the *I Chin Ching* are forgeries, that their terminology gives no indication of Indian origins, and that there is no evidence that Bodhidharma himself wrote anything of the kind. There is in fact nothing known of anything that Bodhidharma did or taught at Shao-lin, except that he is supposed to have sat staring at the wall of his cell for nine years, as a result of which it is rumoured that he became able to hear the conversation of the ants. This in turn has led to rumours that he was probably crazy. In any case, the exercises in the *I Chin Ching* do not themselves at all resemble a method of boxing, although they obviously imply the existence of boxing systems, and systems using the occult force of *ch'i* (*ki* in Japanese.) They are apparently recipes for cultivating *ch'i* and distributing it through the body. They are also very largely incomprehensible, which is at least a partial reason for suspecting that they might have some occult import. The following translations by Dr Smith give an idea of what one is up against:

While holding the *ch'i* down in the lower torso your left hand goes up, your right hand down alternately, your two palms open and flat … inhale and let your *ch'i* sink. Keep your hands close to your legs and draw strength from under your armpits. Your shoulders are held flat like the opened wings of a wild goose. Your heels rise and fall with the shooting out and retracting of your arms.

The more specific are in some ways the more baffling. For example:

Bring your feet together. Keeping normal fists, raise your arms frontally until they parallel shoulders. Using strength, take your arms to the direct side where they are aligned to your shoulders. Your palms are down. Then rise on toes and alternatively stand on the heel of each foot. As you lower toes, exhale and open your fists. Do forty-nine times. This improves the internal environment.

These exercises and ten others of similar style were to be performed in three sets of forty-nine repetitions, night and morning. There is no doubt at all that the main effect of these movements is to inspire the person doing them with the gravest possible doubts. One cannot of course be certain that after raising one's thumbs 147 times night and morning, for example, one will not succeed in training intrinsic force to rise and fall after ten years. Anyone primarily concerned with self-defence might on the other hand feel that this time could well be better spent developing an accurate straight left and swift kick. But these gymnastics attributed by forgers to Bodhidharma are not the only recommended way of acquiring control over intrinsic energy. Their main importance is indeed simply to indicate the existence of a traditional link in China between the martial arts and occult forces, wherever the knowledge of this association might have come from originally.

The rest of the story can be summarized very quickly. In either the fourteenth or the sixteenth century, a man possibly named Yen became priest under the name of Chueh Yuen, and became devoted to the martial arts. In the course of his travels, he met two masters, Li Ch'eng and Pai Yu-feng. They returned with him to the Shao-lin monastery, and there pooled their knowledge to devise a system of 70 self-defence actions, grouped in five distinct styles, called respectively 'dragon', 'snake', 'leopard', 'tiger' and 'crane', because of their supposed resemblance to the movements of the animals in question. More precisely, the boxing master would use his back-fist to strike in the manner of a dragon's thrashing tail; his extended fingers would stab to the eyeballs like a snake's fangs; his open hand would smash out like a tiger's claw; his foreknuckle would twist into an enemy's ribs like a leopard's paw; and his thumb and fingertips pressed together would peck fatally at the throat, like a crane's beak. There was also an occult connotation: the five creatures described represented the five essences of a man's physical powers. Thus, the dragon represented spirit, apparently corresponding here to 'mood', or 'disposition', as in 'good spirits'; the snake represented *ch'i*; the leopard, strength; the tiger, bone; and the crane, sinew. The appropriateness of the symbols might not always be perfectly clear, but it does not really matter.

To resume the narrative, in the seventeenth century, the Shao-lin monks, who had supported the Ming dynasty, were driven out by the Manchus, and their boxing knowledge was thus spread all over the country. Other styles had already developed, which probably owed no more to the styles developed at Shao-lin by Yuen, Li and Pai, than their styles owed to any exercise system developed in the past, wherever that might have come from. In any case, tai-chi ch'uan and hsing-i had appeared as distinctive styles by the eighteenth century, whether derived from Shao-lin or not. Tung Hai-ch'uan learned the art of pa-kua in the nineteenth century from an unknown Taoist monk in Kiangsu, but apparently without keeping any record of where the monk got it from, if anywhere. And that almost brings the story up to date.

At this point, it is necessary to remind the reader that no truer statement has ever been made than Robert W. Smith's warning that 'boxing literature is uneven, full of gaps, and smothered in places by ambiguities'. One really has to abandon any attempt at a connected narrative from here on, and simply record what appear to be a few basic and reliable facts, without regard to order or relationship. The facts are these. There are over one hundred recognized different styles of Chinese boxing in existence today, not counting the assorted schools which teach combat methods with spears, swords, flails and other weapons. Most of these hundred-plus schools do in fact differ very strikingly from one another, although others again seem to be virtually identical. On the other hand, in many cases a recognized different style will itself be taught in different ways by different teachers. One has to accept the fact that the Chinese are a nation of individualists, and there are really about as many different styles of Chinese boxing as there are Chinese boxers, and there may well be all of a million of those. All these various modes of combat are however known by one or other of the two generic names of wu shu, meaning 'martial arts', or kung-fu. The latter and more generally used term has no particular reference to the martial arts. The word *kung* means, as far as the Chinese themselves are able to agree, 'something of a task or piece of work to be accomplished', or words to that general effect. *Fu* means simply 'man'. Most of these styles do indeed seem to have been developed or systematized at the Shao-lin monastery, before the diaspora in the seventeenth century. However, few of the major schools, with the important exception of wing chun kung-fu, seem actually to have originated at Shao-lin; others, such as tai-chi ch'uan, pa-kua, hsing-i, and tong long (praying mantis) certainly seem to have been developed outside the monastery; and none even of those styles associated with Shao-lin can be traced back with the slightest confidence to any system known before the twelfth century. Both boxing and the use of intrinsic energy in boxing appear to antedate any developments known to have occurred at Shao-lin. The term Shao-lin boxing has indeed now come to be applied almost exclusively to the styles of Chinese boxing which are least concerned with intrinsic energy, relying upon normal athletic skill and technique for their effect.

These styles form what the Chinese call the 'hard' style of self-defence. The occult styles which use intrinsic energy to supplement or replace muscular strength are by contrast 'soft'. These terms are of course no more exact than any others in this field of inquiry. A Chinese student, for example, insisted to the writer that aikido, the softest of all soft arts in its total reliance on *ki* and circular movements, was in fact 'not all that soft'. In the same way, wing chun, the hardest of all hard styles in its reliance on sheer technique, was devised by a Buddhist nun as an alternative to the existing hard or 'strong horse' styles of Shao-lin. A more satisfactory distinction is perhaps that between 'external' and 'internal' schools, the former using muscular strength and the latter using intrinsic force.

This of course is not the whole answer either. Most styles of the hard as well as the soft schools do in fact use both muscular strength and intrinsic energy. But it can at least be affirmed, even if one can be sure of nothing else, that tai-chi ch'uan, pa-kua and hsing-i are the soft styles of the internal schools par excellence. Anything that can be learned about occult martial arts of China can be learned from these.

Tai-chi ch'uan is the acknowledged summit of Chinese systems of self-defence. It is indeed almost the only style which practitioners of other styles admit to be any good at all. Almost all Chinese martial artists agree in despising one another. The exceptions are a mutual tolerance among the white crane, praying mantis and wing chun experts, and a common respect for the internal school, and especially for tai-chi ch'uan. There is no doubt that the claims of the latter demand respect, even from those who cannot bring themselves to believe them. Among its benefits are invulnerability in combat, perfect health and long life. It is particularly recommended for all persons suffering from neurasthenia, high blood pressure, anaemia, tuberculosis, gastric and enteric diseases, paralysis, kidney diseases, etc. Anybody suffering from the terminal stages of tuberculosis or heart disease is however cautioned against trying to practise tai-chi ch'uan too hard at the start. Those who have practised it for any length of time certainly stand out in a crowd: we are assured that their cheeks will be a healthy red colour; their temples will be full and swelling; their ears will be crimson; their abdomens will be solid and elastic like drum leather. When they are standing, their two feet will be as firm as if they were stuck in the ground. Their step will be light. Their muscles will be as soft as cotton while the intrinsic energy suffusing them remains inactive; but they will be stiff when intrinsic energy is active.

Pugilistic achievements of the masters of tai-chi ch'uan far exceed anything claimed even for aikido. Cheng Man-ch'ing, author of perhaps the most authoritative as well as comprehensible treatise on tai-chi ch'uan, testifies that his teacher's eldest uncle, while still sound asleep, had kicked a servant who had tried to awaken him as high as the level of the roof. His teacher's father, also while still asleep, had seized and thrown a rat at the wall with such force that it stuck to it. Another member of the same redoubtable family was attacked by a rival boxer, who took the precaution of first blinding him by throwing sand in his eyes. The master nonetheless managed to avoid the attack, and hurl his assailant away 'a distance of several ten feet', which is impressive, however you measure it.

At this stage, the western sceptic would probably prefer a little more concrete and if possible contemporary evidence. There is no problem here. Despite the intense secretiveness pervading all the Chinese martial arts, the masters of tai-chi ch'uan have certainly not hesitated to put on impressive and frequent public performances. Chinese diplomat George K. C. Weh reports having seen a 250-pound western boxer thrown to the ground by a tai-chi master literally less than half his weight. In 1971, sixty-year-old tai-chi ch'uan expert Huang Sheng Hsien humiliated Malaysian wrestling champion Leow Kong Seng, half his age and far heavier, by repeatedly and easily throwing Leow to the ground in a fifteen-minute contest, without once losing balance himself.

It might be pointed out, incidentally, that the term 'throw' is peculiarly exact here. Tai-chi ch'uan does not use conventional methods of grappling and tripping. Nor is an opponent flipped with a wrist-lock, as in aikido. Basically, he presses the attacker's arm away to one side or the other, applies his own hands or wrists to the attacker's body, and simply pushes him up and away, driving off his own rear foot. This is of course in 'friendly' bouts. In actual combat, he hits him at the closest possible range with a vertical fist, or kicks him. Thus, old Cheng Man-ch'ing himself lifts younger and larger opponents several feet off the ground with the back of his wrist, literally throwing them away without any appearance of effort at all, and performs Tohei's feat of repelling the efforts of a number of men to push him off balance, driving them back with his unexerted finger. Tai-chi artists appear in public and even on television, shattering bricks with bare, uncalloused hands, and in particular receiving full-muscled blows on any part of their usually bare bodies, without pain or bruising, and even without any of the preliminary muscular tensing or focusing of physical strength used by karateka in similar demonstrations.

Chan See-meng, winner of a gold medal in the South-East Asia Open Pugilistic Tournament in Singapore in 1969, and at present a respectable bank clerk in Kuala Lumpur, described how he saw Master (Sifu) Yang of the Chin Woo Athletic Association in Kuala Lumpur, repeatedly throw attackers some twenty feet away from them. Sifu Chee himself demonstrates his control of *ch'i* by assuming a meditative posture, sitting cross-legged, while allowing a student to smash a toughened knife-hand blow to the top of his cranium, probably the most dreadfully dangerous blow that one could well expose oneself to. Sifu Chee is still alive and well and teaching boxing in Malaysia. Nor again are these feats in any way unusual. Robert W. Smith found boxers in Taiwan who were perfectly prepared to let Smith punch them with all his strength in the testicles, for the benefit of photographers, thereby apparently proving that one can actually put *ch'i* in the groin, despite John F. Gilbey's assumption that one could not.

Most of these achievements are again quite impossible in conventional physical terms. One just cannot physically resist strength which is far greater than one's own muscles can match; one cannot physically break substances harder than bone with an uncalloused knuckle; one cannot physically allow an athlete to hit one on the relaxed back, the unprotected head or the undefended scrotum with hardwood stave, toughened edge of hand or clenched fist without showing some effects, such as breakage or fatal internal haemorrhage. Something quite unaccountable in physical terms must be going on. But unfortunately even the masters themselves do not seem to be able to explain satisfactorily exactly what they are doing, let alone how they do it. It is not that they are secretive, just that their explanations do not make complete sense. There must presumably be some sequence of cause and effect, even in the sphere of the occult. Thus Sifu Chee says that he includes in his training schedules meditative postures designed to 'activate the

ch'i and make it flow'. These are obviously the same as the
postures adopted in aikido and other forms of kung-fu internal
boxing, where the wrists are tensed, the chest depressed, and
the body lowered into the legendary 'horseback' or half-squat-
ting position. However, Sifu Chee has yet another definition of
ch'i: it is 'the psycho-physiological power associated with
blood, breath and mind'. All one can say is that it may be
associated with them, but it is certainly not just them. Neither
breath nor blood can prevent injury to the mind when the top of
the head is assaulted in the manner described above. In any
case, one would expect logically that breath and blood could at
best produce effects only within the body of the subject doing
the breathing. They could hardly help him to produce effects
on somebody else's body. Yet the claim of the Chinese artist is
precisely that he is able not only to transmit intrinsic energy to
any part of his own body which he wishes to protect against
injury, but also to transmit it effectively to cause injury to
external objects, through punches which have a destructive
force in no way explicable in ordinary terms of body mechanics.

   This at least really cannot be just myth. The ultimate test of
even an occult fighting art must necessarily be its utility in
actual fighting. We have already mentioned the unquestioned
superiority which Chinese masters have demonstrated over
karateka in combat. The Chinese also fight each other with no
less restrained ferocity. And the record of their tournaments
shows that age and physical strength are nothing like as important to them as they are in either western or Japanese styles. Sifu
Buck Sam Kong says that the art of internal boxing requires
nearly a lifetime of practice before its full potential can be
reached: 'A master of kung-fu develops slowly, like a ginger
root. Mild in taste when young, it becomes hotter and spicier
with the passage of time.' Quite certainly, most of the leading
fighters whom Robert W. Smith met with in Taiwan were in
their fifties or early sixties; contestants in the tournaments of
the South-East Asian Pugilistic Association in Singapore are
usually not younger than thirty-plus; Yip Man, the patriarch of
wing chun kung-fu, probably the fastest of all systems of self-

defence, is in his seventies; and kung-fu masters in their sixties and seventies fight and win in the open tournaments now revived in Hong Kong. All the evidence is that the use of intrinsic energy is indeed mastered progressively with age, and that its mastery enables one to dispense with simple physical strength.

What of course does take a little explanation is how masters of internal boxing actually manage to defeat one another, seeing that all alike are presumably able to use intrinsic energy to protect themselves against injury, and at the same time inflict immensely powerful blows upon opponents. It would seem literally to be a case of immovable objects contending with irresistible forces. There is ample testimony that novices repeatedly find themselves simply unable either to hurt masters with whom they are fighting, or to prevent the masters from hurting them. But this does not explain how the masters defeat one another. One can only say that it seems to be entirely a question of the degree of mastery. Nobody can master *ch'i* completely while he still has a physical body. All mastery is thus imperfect, but some have advanced in its use more than others. *Ch'i* may be able to make a man invulnerable and irresistible if he were able to develop it fully, but nobody can develop it fully so long as it has to operate within the confines of the physical universe.

That at least seems to be the case. In the meantime, all one can do is recognize that technique is everything, even though the greatest technician can of necessity attain only limited control over the *ch'i*. One thing for which we can be grateful is that the techniques of Chinese boxing have now been revealed to a sufficient degree for us to know what we are dealing with. Only a tiny number of the hundred-odd styles have indeed been publicized, but one can reasonably assume that these are the ones which the Chinese themselves regard as the most significant.

The first thing to be said about them, on the most practical level, is that their methods are in general utterly unlike those of either karate or western boxing. There is a family resemblance to aikido in posture, foot-work and the way in which both hands are used simultaneously, though the general impression is far more aggressive, simply because aikido is primarily a grappling art, and Chinese boxing a striking one. But its mode of striking is utterly individual. Karate, as explained already, punches in a straight line, but with the punching hand and arm drawn back as far as they will go, to gain maximum momentum by allowing for the full expansion and contraction of the muscles of the punching arm. Every karate blow is delivered in a state of maximum physical tension. Western boxing by contrasts favours relaxation of the body until the moment of impact, and theoretically prefers to use punches which travel as short a distance as possible, but attempts to enhance their impact by rolling the weight of the body behind the punch. In fact, of course, the most consistently hard hitters in western boxing have achieved their most impressive knock-downs with either long, overhand rights, or with even longer, partially-swung left hooks, both of which cover the greatest distance possible before reaching their target.

It is the peculiar feature of Chinese boxing that it uses neither technique. Chinese punches are either enormously long but comparatively slow looping straight-arm swings, or else incredibly short arm movements delivered without any kind of shoulder roll or rise off the back foot, to add bodyweight to the punch. It in other words delivers punches of terrifying effectiveness with physical movements which western boxing would tend to dismiss as essentially ineffective, or even impossible.

As always, one has to be a little careful here. Effectiveness in hitting comes from either impact or penetration. A thrust from a rapier or a stiletto can penetrate a human body sufficiently easily to do fatal damage, even when the point is actually against the skin. A boxer on the other hand needs distance to generate impact, because fists cannot penetrate. However, certain forms of striking against certain vulnerable points of the body do not actually require much impact to be effective. The classic foreknuckle strike of the praying mantis school against rib cage or external obliques can paralyse an opponent with very little force, simply because the power behind the blow is

concentrated in a very small striking area against a very deli-
cate target. It is equivalent to a thrust with a blunt knife. A
praying mantis boxer can accordingly hit with great effect from
a distance of perhaps eight inches, without any occult as-
sistance.

In the same way, Sifu Buck Sam Kong explains that many of
the techniques do not require maximum power. A two-fingered
strike to the eyes or a leopard's hand to the throat could disable
anyone. Indeed, Masutatsu Oyama has grimly warned against
striking to the eyes with excessive force, because of the
difficulty one might otherwise experience in withdrawing one's
fingers. Similarly, wing chun boxers twist their wrists upwards
at the moment of impact, snapping the lower knuckles of the
fist against the opponent's chin or body to generate an explosive
impact without the use of shoulder or body-weight. Praying
mantis boxers use an extraordinary but by no means unknown
form of muscular control, tightening the muscles above the
shoulder blade to produce the same effect. But once again, the
results produced appear to be out of all proportion to the physical means used to produce them. Masutatsu Oyama reports
how elderly Chinese boxers simply walk up to arrangements of
bricks and tiles and shatter them with apparently light, uncon-
sidered blows with uncalloused hands, without any of the preliminary breathing, posturing, kiai-yelling and enormous
muscular exertion of karate. Anthony Curtis describes how
Serge Martich-Osterman, demonstrating internal punching 'sat
back and closed his eyes, and his right hand came floating over,
ever so gently, and his knuckles brushed my arm. Whack! The
arm jerked back and I spun out of the chair. The table rocked
and the beer glasses crashed to the floor.' Rolf Clausnitzer recounts his experience in taking 'a nine-inch punch from Wong
Shun Leong, one of the few wing chun masters in Hong Kong
today. Despite the protection of two cushions, the memory
remains of an excruciating pain not unlike that of an electric
shock.'

Finally, John F. Gilbey describes the effect of the hsing-i cork-

screw punch, delivered by English Professor William Fuller
from within three inches of the opponent's midriff, and 'with no
appreciable thought of strength'. According to Dr Gilbey: 'He
went into the basic stance and caressed me with his right fist.
The effect was instantaneous. I bent over and retched. I had not
eaten for several hours, otherwise I would have tossed it all
then and there.'

Most convincingly perhaps, Bruce Lee demonstrated in
public, before photographers, his capacity to deliver a punch of
tremendous impact, standing right foot forward, with his
almost fully-extended right arm an inch away from his partner,
who, like Mr Clausnitzer, held a heavily-padded glove against
his chest for protection. In this position, from which it is physically impossible to generate enough power to hurt an opponent,
Lee knocked his partner flying into a waiting chair, several feet
behind him.

After demonstrations of this kind, one sees no reason to
doubt the claim of tai-chi exponents to be able to hit with
complete effectiveness from a distance of six inches, or even
when their fists are actually in contact with the body of the
opponent, since what is seen to happen bears no relationship to
physical mechanics. The only explanations again are fraud or
intrinsic force, though it is really hard to see how there can be
that many liars around.

This is particularly the case with tai-chi, which is by far the
most advertised mystery in the world. Enormously detailed
books on tai-chi have been available in English since before the
war. English fashion magazines recommended it in the fifties as
a means of calming the mind and slimming the body. Glossy
American hardbacks present in the same manner, frequently in
company with a summary of the *I Chin Ching*, so that one can
learn physical poise, mental enlightenment and the art of for-
tune-telling, all from the one book.

This popular appeal has in many ways only added to the
mystery of tai-chi ch'uan. The most dedicated students of intrinsic force are undoubtedly the martial artists, and even
Oriental martial artists have occasionally observed tai-chi

ch'uan drills being practised, drawn the conclusion that a
system involving windmill-like arm movements performed as
slowly as humanly possible was clearly useless as a means of
self-defence against anything more formidable than an angry
mosquito, and gone back to screaming at themselves and breaking tiles.

They were gravely mistaken in doing so. But their error was
positively fostered by the Chinese, ever secretive about their
own most significant discoveries. The fact is that there are two
aspects of tai-chi ch'uan. There is the actual combat system,
which uses the shortest blows in the world with terrific speed
and economy, and there is the system of calisthenics, which
uses the longest movements with what appears to be the greatest possible wastage of time and effort. For example, one of the
more direct recommended responses to a simple frontal attack,
given in a book on the practical applications of tai-chi ch'uan,
begins:

... turn the upper part of the body and your two hands to the
right, so that you face the north. The centre of gravity is shifted
to the right foot. Stop your left hand before the forehead. Clench
your right hand into a fist and make it circle downward a half
vertical round in front of your chest, the knuckles facing north.
Lean the upper part of the body to the left. The centre of gravity
is shifted to the left foot. Raise your right fist and make it circle
to the right one vertical round and stop again in front of your
chest, the knuckles facing upward. Lean the upper part of the
body first to the right and then to the left. The centre of gravity is
shifted first to the right foot and then back to the left. The left
hand stands still, but makes a small vertical circle, following the
momentum of your body ...

A further fifteen movements follow before the response is completed.

This is clearly not a combat art. Anybody who has seen tai-
chi performed as a self-defence system soon realizes that the
movements of combat tai-chi bear in fact only a faint resemblance to the 128 movements of tai-chi calisthenics. The
latter are indeed only preparations for the former. Their pur-

pose is to train balance and coordination, perfection of form, and to cultivate and direct intrinsic energy.

Here indeed is where it all begins. The name 'tai-chi' itself can be translated as 'Grand Ultimate'. This term refers in the *I Chin Ching* to the 'changeless absolute behind the phenomenon of change'. It can also be described as 'Ultimate Nothingness', if that is any easier to conceive. The theory is that Ultimate Nothingness generates the two primary forces of the *Yin* and the *Yang*. These forces represent respectively, darkness and light, softness and firmness, the ends of creation and the beginnings of creation, inactivity and activity, female and male, obedience and strength, insubstantiality and substantiality, negative and positive, retreat and advance. Ultimate Nothingness becomes creative as *yang*. When creation reaches the extreme point, it becomes passive as *yin*. Extreme inactivity in its turn brings on creativity again. The process of action and reaction is ceaseless, as all things are being reproduced eternally.

These groupings may not seem entirely obvious. It is for example not easy to see why darkness should be associated with softness, although it is gratifying to note that tai-chi clearly recognizes a female as well as a male principle in divinity, and makes them not only mutually indispensable, but equal in importance, since one cannot operate without the other. It is not surprising that Women's Liberationists find Asian theology more gratifying than European.

This mutual interdependence of the *yin* and the *yang* is expressed in the famous 'double fish' diagram, inscribed on the banners of most kung-fu schools, in which two identical forms, one white and one black, occupy equal areas in a circle, the white form containing a black element, and the black containing a white one. A rather more complicated diagram of black and white circles by Chou Lien-ch'i conveys the same idea of equipoise. It was a considerably more complex view of the universe than the simple basic notion of aikido, that the love of God is the fundamental source of the martial arts.

One might however suggest tentatively that the two ideas are only different ways of saying the same thing, namely, that all things are created by Divine Consciousness, and that it is the nature of Divine Consciousness to be eternally creative. It is of course something else again to explain why or how Divine Consciousness should be creative. One can only suggest feebly that consciousness is will, and will is what creates. But this need not worry us too much. After all, we have no idea how our own wills work, and we have absolutely no idea how anything supernatural works, if there is anything supernatural to work.

There are a lot of other things that we do not know either. Norman Mailer has pointed out that we can measure the force of gravitational attraction, but we do not know why bodies are attracted to each other, any more than we know what energy looks like; what electricity is; why passing a wire between the poles of a horseshoe magnet should cause an electrical current to run through the wire; what the nature of time is; why certain waves make a sound in the ear; or how light travels.[1] Science has really quite a way still to go.

So a little more mystery hardly matters. What is important here is to learn how the principles of tai-chi can be utilized to open one's physical body to the powers of intrinsic energy. The basic concept is the identity of the human being with Ultimate Nothingness, of the created with the creator, of the physical world with the cosmos. Intrinsic energy provides the link, as the factor present in all. If we are pictures in the mind of Divine Nothingness, then we possess with Divine Nothingness the creative energies which pictured us. Intrinsic energy is inherent in man, just as it is in God. What is necessary is for us to adapt and dispose our physical bodies and brains so that they offer the least impediment to the movements of intrinsic energy. This is reasonably easy to understand, whether one agrees with the idea or not. Some tai-chi theorists, however, go a little further, insisting on a very practical identification of the human individual with Ultimate Nothingness, by arguing that the body is itself a tai-chi = Grand Terminus = Ultimate Nothingness; that nothing could be more specific than the directions for performing the movements of tai-chi ch'uan nor the reasons for doing them in the manner prescribed. One's objective is to throw every bone and muscle of the entire body open as a thoroughfare for the *ch'i*.

One accordingly begins by standing in a position of total relaxation. The head is erect, as if supported by a cord from the ceiling, the spine straight, the eyes looking straight ahead, the mind empty of all thoughts, the mouth closed, the tongue pressed lightly against the palate, shoulders lowered and chest depressed. One's bearing is thus in many ways the opposite of that prescribed by western drill instructors.

The purpose of this upright but relaxed stance is to allow such *ch'i* as one possesses already to sink to a point one and one-third inches below the navel. Eventually the *ch'i* collecting in this place begins to overflow and circulate through the body. It also generates heat, which congeals when it cools, as marrow on the inner pores of the bones of the spinal column. This heat also evaporates excess water in the stomach and intestines. The effect of the circulation of *ch'i* is to make one's limbs feel at once light and filled with power, floating in the air as those of a swimmer float in the water. The sensation or illusion of floating is intensified by the intensely slow and rhythmical nature of the movements, 'as slow and even as the chewing of food'. Persons performing the movements individually or in public usually remain in the initial relaxed standing posture until they become aware of the movement of *ch'i* within their bodies, before actually beginning to move. The movements themselves begin from the 'bubbling well spring', an internal aperture situated in the feet, suitable for acupuncture therapy. Hence the traditional sayings that 'boxing is rooted in the feet' and 'strength is shot out of the legs as an arrow is from the bow.'

All this as always is quite a lot to take on trust. The anatomical illustrations in particular do not help much to convince. One cannot really prove that any of the processes described are really going on, and the fact that one can very soon sense the experiences of warm lightness and floating attributed to the circulation of *ch'i* is not itself evidence, since one can usually persuade oneself that one can feel anything one expects to feel wherever one expects to feel it. Again, one has to distinguish between exercises which are simply good for one in a normal physical sense, and those which claim to be rituals for the acquiring of more than physical powers. Tai-chi ch'uan is necessarily good for one. It develops relaxation, calms the nerves, improves the posture, and cultivates muscular coordination. The fact that has been shown again and again is that it also, in some cases at least, imparts to its practitioners a capacity to exert or resist force which is not explicable in terms of any physical benefit it might have done them. Perhaps the *ch'i* really does move up from the bubbling well spring, as one thinks one can feel it doing.

Tai-chi shares with aikido the basic principles of total relaxation and harmonious movement, and the avoidance of obvious physical exertion, including shouting or forceful exhalation. It differs from aikido in its far greater emphasis on striking, in its use of pushing rather than twisting to fell an opponent, and in its far more explicit idea of what is meant by the key term. There is no possibility of interpreting *ch'i* as anything but intrinsic energy, while one of the difficulties in the way of coming to grips with the concept of *ki* is the fact that the term is used to mean concepts like momentum, intention and breath force, as well as intrinsic energy. It also resembles very closely indeed the two other great schools of 'internal boxing', pa-kua, described by Robert W. Smith as 'unlike and superior to' the other boxing arts, and the almost totally unknown hsing-i, hailed by Gilbey as 'the highest form of the boxing art'.[2] Both these schools insist like tai-chi on the need to avoid using excessive muscular strength to achieve identification with the universe, and to develop intrinsic force by the cultivation of *ch'i*. This is done in both cases by the practice of 'quiet standing', as described in the section on tai-chi ch'uan, followed by the slow performance of harmonious circling movements.

There are interesting and illuminating differences, however. The movements of tai-chi are ideally performed in a condition of relaxation amounting virtually to a trance, or sleep-walking. The movements of pa-kua at least are performed in a state of muscular tension which must approximate uncommonly to the experience of being on the rack. As Robert W. Smith unforgettably translates, when you start to move in pa-kua,

that area of the hand from the tip of the thumb to the tip of the index finger is opened like a crescent and pushes forward slightly. Bend the tips of your little fingers and ring fingers, hooking them downward. As you hold your palms away from you, you must *feel* that they are trying to turn inward towards you (the wrists are turning upwards). The main strength of your left arm is contracted or withdrawn, and that of your rear hand is pushing outward and expanding ... In contracting your trapezius muscles your right arm should be close to your body. Your back should be slightly bowed forward and tight as a drum ... Both shoulders contract and both elbows point down. As your palms turn, imagine some resistance. While circling, your waist turns in the opposite direction of your hands – like twisting a rope. As you walk, the back of your thighs contracts upward towards your sacrum; and your inner thighs contract both inward and outward towards your groin.

Dr Smith comments truly that: 'It comes down to the fact that in the beginning pa-kua will seem the antithesis of the relaxed and natural boxing it is said to be ... An hour of pa-kua walking equates to at least an hour of the most strenuous sport known to man.'

The achievement of *ch'i* through agony is indeed at least as basic in Chinese tradition as its achievement through ease and relaxation. Early kung-fu systems of the internal school required their novices to adopt the famous 'horseback stance', squatting slightly with legs apart and back rounded as if sitting on a horse, for periods of up to two hours. This would feel not so much like being on the rack as being burned alive. Sifu Buck Sam Kong, now living in Hawaii, records that the first six months of his initial training in Hong Kong were devoted entirely to mastering the horse stance. 'A stick of incense, timed to burn for forty-five minutes, was placed in front of the student. He was expected to maintain the stance until the incense had burned out. In the beginning this training was not only dull, but also extremely painful.'

One purpose of this torture was of course simply to strengthen the legs, and give stability to the boxer. The more esoteric reason was to expel useless or stale energy from the lower part of the body, so that intrinsic energy might accumulate uninterrupted. Another reason of course was simply to make the system more exclusive. Praying mantis boxers complacently boast today that no occidental would have the self-discipline to endure the preliminary training. Nor is this emphasis on physical endurance confined to the rougher 'strong horse' schools. Masters of internal boxing schools, including those teaching tai-chi, are perfectly likely to strike students or slap their faces to induce a right spirit within them. Zen meditation periods are supervised by proctors who strike meditators on the back and shoulder with wooden staves if they suspect that their concentration is slipping. People who have their powers of concentration aided by being hammered in this way testify that the experience is refreshing and agreeable, which proves that one can get used to anything. A Japanese master swordsman would similarly instil alertness in his students by leaping at them and assaulting them whenever he could do so unobserved. No student could ever be fully certain that the next moment would not bring his sensei landing on his head with a wooden sword. After a few months of this hell upon earth, the pupil would either have become a complete mental wreck or would have acquired the same virtually clairvoyant alertness that the sensei was possessed of.

The other vitally important feature of pa-kua and hsing-i is that pa-kua pretends to be based entirely upon circling motion, but in fact relies on straightforward motion for its most effective moves; while hsing-i both pretends to be and is based upon direct, straightforward, 'vertical' motion. The hsing-i master parries and strikes while moving forward against his opponent, just as the wing chun boxer or karateka does. So indeed does the tai-chi ch'uan master, when he is fighting rather than developing *ch'i*. The movements of tai-chi calisthenics are as roundabout and expansive as those of a broadsword player. Those of combat tai-chi are as fast and economical as a rapier thrust.

There is no more need to recount the legendary achievements of pa-kua and hsing-i boxers than there is to dismiss
them all. You only need one miracle, after all. Sight and feeling
are the only evidence one can use in an inquiry like this, and too
many reliable people have seen and felt too many Chinese
boxers, aikidoists and even karateka perform deeds which could
not have been performed by normal physical strength. What
does emerge from a study of the fighting arts of Asia is that
these qualities are not fraudulent, freakish or arbitrarily dis-
posed. They are, on the other hand, capable of being acquired
through training, just as athletic skills can be acquired through
training. This does not mean to say that everybody who trains
in this way will be successful in acquiring occult powers, any
more than it means that everybody who trains as a sprinter will
necessarily become able to run a hundred yards in ten seconds.
Much must depend on the physical, mental and psychic qualities possessed by the novice to begin with. But it does mean
that the occult powers of Asian martial artists are quite capable
of being termed 'normal' in the sense that anyone has an even
chance of acquiring them, if he works hard enough or long
enough; and it does mean that there are set procedures for
acquiring these powers. The procedures do indeed differ, especially in the demands they make upon the novice, but again
they have obvious principles in common. One does not acquire
intrinsic energy, so much as render oneself ready to receive it.
One does this by above all composing one's body, banishing
distractions from the mind, identifying oneself with the universe, by cultivating a mood of personal unconcern which para-
doxically involves a heightening of awareness, and by believing
in the *ch'i* and waiting for it to move.

This may sound not unlike certain religious exercises of the
Christian faith, but it is only to be expected, if only because
certain of the Christian saints or martyrs are claimed to have
demonstrated similar capacity to disregard what might be
termed the forces of nature. Padre Pio's convincingly attested
ability to appear in different places at the same time, St Joseph
of Cupertino's performances of levitation and Archbishop
Cranmer's action at his execution of holding his right hand in

the flames until it was burned off, might reasonably be described as being in the same category of human achievement as the Chinese boxer who repeatedly slipped behind John F. Gilbey, without Gilbey's being able to see where he went; the pa-kua boxer at the turn of the century who supported a Sumo wrestler on his outstretched arm; of the tai-chi boxers who absorb relaxedly blows with hardwood poles. They are all doing the same kind of thing. The difference is that the Asiatics did not acquire these abilities as an incidental by-product of their acceptance of certain religious dogmas. They knew what they were doing. They trained their bodies and minds to become avenues for intrinsic energy. They did yoga.

5 The way of yoga:
Indian, Tibetan

Indian yoga

All occult experience involving the subjection of physical laws to the power of the will, or more simply mind over matter, can be described as yoga, in the grammatically accurate sense of the word. The term 'yoga' itself is derived from the root *yuj*, meaning 'union'. The union which the adept, or yogi, seeks, is of course union with God. Bhakti Yogi Maharaj Charan Singhji of Beas has said that yoga is simply 'spiritual practice for God realization'. This of course is itself not the easiest of concepts to grasp. It is literally true that many libraries have been filled with books written to explain what is meant by 'God realization'. This is perhaps no more remarkable than the fact that almost all the immeasurable mass of creative writing produced by mankind has been concerned with the depiction or analysis of love. There are some subjects one does not get tired of. Nor is there any doubt that it takes a lot of words to define the indefinable. But it does mean that anybody attempting to write about yoga is faced with appalling problems. There is really no way of knowing when to stop. One cannot use too many words or too few when writing about the most extensive and most important of human experiences.

Two preliminary remarks at least have to be made. One is that there are formally at least a number of different forms of yoga. The most fundamental and also comprehensible distinction is that between raja-yoga ('royal' or 'classical' yoga) which is concerned with the yoga of mind-control ('laya-yoga'), and hatha-yoga, which is most obviously if not most importantly a system of exercises for physical improvement. The distinction is no more clear-cut and final than anything else in this business, because hatha-yoga aims at spiritual enlightenment just as raja-yoga does, and raja-yoga employs some of the easier physical postures and principles of hatha-yoga as aids to enlightenment. Raja-yoga itself can then be divided into what appears to be as many forms as one likes. The point here really seems to be that the different forms represent merely different shades of emphasis, rather than significantly different styles, in much the same way as one could suggest that hsing-i, pa-kua and tai-chi ch'uan are identical for at least four parts of the time, and that in practice all three become virtually indistinguishable from the more efficient styles of kung-fu, and so on.

However, the most familiar subdivisions of raja-yoga are karma-yoga, jnana-yoga, bhakti-yoga and perhaps kundalini-yoga. Karma-yoga implies selfless activity, the dedication of one's life's work to the idea of God: it is thus concerned primarily with action. Jnana-yoga is the yoga of wisdom and learning, having as its end the mystic experience of the revelation of God: it 'aims at the realization of the unique and supreme self ... by the method of intellectual reflection ... to right discrimination':[1] it is the yoga of the intellect. Bhakti-yoga is the yoga of devotion or love, through which it is claimed virtually 'all the great and famous Indian saints ... have declared from the housetops that they have, through the sheer force of devotion, compelled the impersonal Brahman to be a personal God, and enjoyed His company, wherever and whenever they liked'; it seeks 'the enjoyment of the Supreme Lord and Bliss and normally utilizes the conception of the Supreme Lord in his personality as the divine lover and enjoyer of the universe.' Finally, one might list kundalini-yoga, the yoga concerned with the development of what is called psychic-nerve force, which can only be yet another term for intrinsic energy, and which employs among other techniques those of yantra-yoga, which employs geometrical diagrams of mystical significance, and mantra-yoga, the yoga of what the West understands

as 'auto-suggestion', with its ritualistic reiteration of words or
sounds of occult power. In practice, as always, all the forms
described above seem to use much the same methods, and undoubtedly all are directed to the same ultimate end of enlightenment, understanding, or if one prefers union with God.
However, the terms are used with such frequency that one
cannot well understand anything about yoga without at least
being aware of their meaning, and the distinctions they are supposed to represent.

The second point that really needs to be emphasized is that
there is nothing arbitrary about the nature of the God who is to
be realized by yoga. Nor is there anything dogmatic about what
realizing Him actually means for the person concerned. One
thing which seems to be attested to more satisfactorily than
anything else in this business by those who claim to have had
the desired mystical experiences, is that he who succeeds in
having visions of God to reward his attempts at realization, will
see God in exactly the form which he expects to see Him in.
Indeed, the purpose behind the striking representations of the
Gods in Indian art, is exactly to insure that the mystic will
know that he is genuinely seeing God and not merely having an
hallucination. Thus any valid vision of Krishna must have four
arms and hands. Dattatreya must have three heads and six
hands, Ganapati must have an elephant's head and four hands,
and Laxmi must have eight or more hands. Dr Vishnu
Mahadeo Bhat of the Institute of Indian Culture in Bombay
explains that this is so as not 'to give the slightest room for
doubt about the objectivity of God's personality . . .'[2]

Again, one does not want to argue, but it might seem reasonable to suggest that all this indicates a vision is in the literal
sense a creation of the visionary, called into being by the conscious or unconscious operation of his will, using the powers of
intrinsic energy which he has made himself receptive to. There
may be considerable more truth than one might have expected
in Oscar Wilde's remark that 'an honest God's the noblest work
of man'. Dr Bhat's argument might be more convincing if
mystics were actually to experience visions of God in forms

which they did not expect, such as the nasty young man with fair hair described by Kingsley Amis in *The Green Man*.[3] It is however certain that in the majority of cases the situation is as described by Swami Chidananda of the Sivananda Ashram: '... If he [the Yogi] is a *bhakta* of Lord Rama, his visions shall be associated with Lord Rama ... If he is a devotee of Lord Krishna, his vision will be of Lord Krishna.'

In the same way, of course, a Christian mystic will see Christ, the Virgin Mary, or whatever saint he is making the particular object of his devotion; and a Moslem will see angels, saints and prophets. This is not exactly saying that dogmatic religion is irrelevant. One's religious beliefs will certainly determine the nature of one's realization of God. But the fact is that the realization takes place as a creation of the imagination of the mystic. It is the technique that is important, not the system of theology that justifies it. As Swami Chidananda says: 'Yoga is above religion.' In the same way, Morihei Uyeshiba insisted that aikido was not a religion, but was at the basis of all religions. Both are in fact preaching the same faith. It is that the ultimate objective is 'union with the world-soul', or perhaps more accurately, becoming fully aware of the identity of the world-soul with oneself, realizing oneself as a manifestation of the world-soul, in just the same way as a master of aikido or internal Chinese boxing opens himself to the movement of the *ki*, or *ch'i*, from which he takes his own origin.

The most satisfactory description of yoga may thus well be that of Professor Evans-Wentz, in his book *Tibetan Yoga*: 'Yoga is the shortest path to the higher evolution of man.'[4] This however is about as far as one can go without qualification. Yoga, like the occult martial arts, can apparently lead to the acquisition by the adept of powers which are not subject to the laws of physical nature. These powers are acquired by making oneself receptive to the free movement of intrinsic energy. This comes in both through the cultivation of the appropriate physical and mental disposition, involving an appreciation of the fact that 'consciousness is permeating all', in the words of Dr Bhat. Opening oneself completely to

Ultimate Nothingness would naturally mean that one knew all things, as well as having the power to do all things. This is exactly what is claimed in the list of yogic perfections, compiled by the sage Patanjali some 2,500 years ago. They include, for instance, wealth unsought, virility, perfect health, clairvoyance, understanding of the language of animals, telepathy, invisibility, precognition, full knowledge of the physical sciences, the ability to enter others' bodies, levitation, aura, telekinesis, power to touch the moon and the stars, mastery over the whole creation, and multiple personality.

Not even the sufis of internal boxing have ever claimed quite so much. However, it is reassuring to discover that the basic mechanics involved are the same in both yoga and the occult martial arts. Occult powers manifest themselves in consequence of the yogi's ability to raise the *kundalini* or intrinsic energy from its resting position, between the anus and the sexual organs, until it reaches the crown of the head, and then lower it again, in preparation for a renewed elevation. This would seem to correspond sufficiently to the process by which the adept of internal boxing learns to allow his *ch'i* (intrinsic energy) to rise from its *tan-tien* (fallow field) approximately three inches below his navel, suffusing his whole body, so that he becomes able to direct it to wherever he wishes. One must however admit that this description of the yogic process may well be a distorting oversimplification of something that can be made to sound unbelievably complex, when crouched in technical or esoteric language. Consider for example this passage from the *Saktanandata-rangini*, quoted by Arthur Avalon (John Woodroffe, *The Serpent Power*, London, 1919):

Knowing that the time for the *prana* (breath, spirit, insubstantial essence that pervades the universe when manifested as rhythmical pulsation which constitutes life) to depart is approaching, and glad that he is about to be absorbed into *Brahman* (world-soul) the yogi sits in *yogasana* (posture suitable for meditation) and restrains his breath by *kumbhaka* (inhaling for a certain time). He then leads the *jivatman* (soul) in the heart to the *muladhara* (inner point, centre, vital region, *centrum*) and by

contracting the anus and following other prescribed processes
arouses *kundalini* (insubstantial substance which pervades the
universe when manifested in the physical body = intrinsic energy
in one form, as *prana* = intrinsic energy in another form). He
then meditates upon the lightning-like blissful *nada* (spiritual
force by which intrinsic energy operates) which is thread-like
and whose substance is *kundalini*. He then merges the *hansa* (the
'self') which is the *Paramatman* (supreme soul) in the form of
prana, in the *nada*, and lead it with the *jiva* through the different
cakras (centres through which intrinsic energy travels in the
body; also psychic nerves in which intrinsic energy is stored in
the body, as electricity is stored or generated in dynamos) to the
rules of *cakrabheda* according to *Ajna-cakra*. He there dissolves
all the diverse elements from the gross to the subtle, beginning
with *Prthivi*, in *kundalini*. Last of all he unifies *Her* (*kundalini*)
and the *jivatman* with the *bindu* (lotus-symbol) whose substance
is *Siva* (pure knowledge) and *Sakti* (supreme energy) which
having done, he pierces the *brahmarandhra* and leaves the body
and becomes merged in the *Brahman*.[5]

This should be esoteric enough for anybody. At the same
time, certain analogies with internal boxing obviously suggest
themselves. *Siva* and *Sakti* as the original elements which com-
bine for the creative process, correspond to the *Yin* and the
Yang. The form of meditation in which the yogi views his body
as a schematic representation of the Universe, corresponds to
the argument in internal boxing that the human body can be
viewed as a tai-chi. Moreover, the yogi may adopt as meditative postures either the relaxed attitudes of raja-yoga or the
spectacular and exacting contortions of hatha-yoga in the same
way that the internal boxer may seek to develop intrinsic
energy through the effortless graceful relaxation of tai-chi
ch'uan, or the physical tortures of pa-kua. Nor is there any
doubt in either art as to where the action is supposed to be.
Yoga, like internal boxing, like kiai-jutsu, like shorinji kempo,
like aikido, like the more esoteric aspects of judo and karate, is
really seeking to achieve a state of undisturbed mental detachment and bodily repose, in which conciousness is centred
in a region below the navel (*muladhara, tanden, tan-tien*) in the

hope that intrinsic energy will radiate from there throughout the body, and ultimately be directed from there to wherever the adept wants it to go. There can be no doubt at all that it is the same process that is being described. In the words of Sri Aurobindo, it is a question of the

conscious centres and sources of all the dynamic powers of our being organizing their action through the plexuses and arranged in an ascending series from the lowest physical to the highest mind centre, and spiritual centre called the thousand-petalled lotus, where ascending Nature, the Serpent Power of the Tantrics, meets the Brahman and is liberated into the Divine Being. These centres are closed or half-closed within us and have to be opened before their full potentiality can be manifested in our physical nature . . .

He also talks about all life being a 'secret yoga, and obscure growth of Nature towards the discovery and fulfillment of the Divine Principle hidden in her'.

The difficulty here, as always, is to be sure exactly what among these terms are to be taken as metaphors, and what literally. This may not be too difficult to analyse. There is no doubt that *kundalini* (serpent-power) is simply an image for the notion of intrinsic energy coiled like a serpent in the lower parts of the body, waiting to uncoil itself; just as the *tan-tien* is a metaphor for intrinsic energy lying as it were fallow, waiting to germinate. One might also assume that the boiling process described in tai-chi ch'uan is just an image for the way in which intrinsic energy transforms the physical nature of the body in which it is developing.

But it is just as clear that not everything is supposed to be metaphor. There is an actual physical process which is supposed to be happening. The simplest way of conceiving it is to imagine intrinsic energy being drawn into the body through the breath. It is then drawn into the lower abdomen, where it is stored in the lowest of the seven centres of the body in which intrinsic energy is accumulated. This is apparently located in the perineum. Intrinsic energy then rises to and is stored in the second of the nerve-centres, in the region of the sexual organs.

It then ascends to the third nerve-centre, about the navel; the fourth, in the heart; the fifth, in the throat; the sixth, the pineal gland or third eye, behind the forehead; and finally into the seventh nerve-centre, the brain. The actual passage through which it ascends is supposed to be a canal in the spinal column, which intrinsic energy enters at the base of the spine.[6] This in the most matter-of-fact language seems to be at basis what the Asians believe is going on.

Even some of this may be only metaphor. But what there can be no argument about is that we find in all these oriental arts a deadly serious theory of physical culture, in which the human body is prepared to serve as a material channel for a force which cannot be material itself, in any normal sense of the term, but which can and does operate in the material world. Moreover, if it is not subject to the ordinary laws of physics, it is certainly limited in this area of operation by the physical and mental disposition of the person cultivating it. To quote Sri Aurobindo again: 'The transforming agent will be bound and stopped in its work by the physical organism's unalterable limitations and held up by the unmodified or imperfectly modified animal within us.' More simply perhaps, Dr Bhat says: 'As long as the yogi has a body, necessarily bodily limitations bind him.' This is not really the same as the Christian idea of original sin: it is just recognizing the logical fact that forces originating from outside the material universe are hindered in their operations in the physical universe by the very nature of the medium they are operating in.

Where the techniques of yoga do seem to differ in a significant degree from those of the martial arts is primarily in their emphasis on breath-control. We have of course already considered the absolutely primary importance attributed to correct breathing in kiai-jutsu, aikido and Chinese boxing. But the emphasis does seem to be quite different from that which one meets in yoga. Admittedly, neither the martial artist nor the yogis seem wholly consistent. The martial artist certainly attempt to use breath-control in a simple physical way as an aid to endurance and speed, trying to hit several times on the one exhalation, in contrast with the karateka, who customarily expends all his reserve breath with each punch. But breathing is also the means by which the *ch'i* is cultivated. This, as we have seen, does not necessarily amount to saying that the breath is the *ch'i*, nor even that the *ch'i* is necessarily inhaled with the breath. The basic reality seems to be that a body which is composed to breathe in the prescribed manner is a body which is also receptive to the *ch'i* and open to its movement. Intrinsic energy comes in a mood of mindless concentration, and a mood of mindless concentration is best induced by deliberate abdominal breathing in a certain posture. Here again John F. Gilbey may well have the last word: the *ch'i* will come when the mood is right, and so long as the mood is right it may not matter what the posture is. On the other hand, it may. We still have to find out.

But the emphasis in yoga breath-control is clearly different in some way. In the first place, breath-control seems to be all-important, while in the martial arts it can only be a means to an end. Dr Bhat asserts categorically that: union with the World-Soul, which is the true and only end of yoga, 'is to be achieved through faith, enthusiasm, memory, concentration and effort ... and the practice of breath-control.' It is apparently the breath itself which is important. Dr P. H. Pott says in *Yoga and Yantra*, (Martinus Nijhoff, The Hague, 1966) that: 'The breath is considered as the material basis of the self, the link between soul and body, and thus as what is most essential to the bodily substance.' Not even the most convinced sceptic is likely to quarrel with the last part of this statement. Breathing is good for you. However, yoga does seem to regard the breath far more emphatically than the martial artists do as being literally intrinsic energy itself. Thus Swami Krishnananda says: '*Prana* (breath) is the force operating in the whole world ... *prana* is universal force ... electric force is a manifestation of *prana* ...' It is in fact pointed out that the life-giving part of the air is really not oxygen but *prana*, so *prana* is definitely equated with the notion of intrinsic energy. But as against that Dr Bhat says: 'Control of *chitta* (mind, ego, intellect, soul) is the only means for yoga' and that concentrated *chitta* can control everything, from the infinitesimal to the infinite. So *chitta* appears to equate to intrinsic energy. In any case, if the *prana* were in fact intrinsic energy, one could only assume that the more we had of it the better, so that one would expect the emphasis in yoga to be on breathing more, not less.

However, Dr Evans-Wentz (*Tibetan Yoga and Secret Doctrines*, OUP, 1951) seems to think that this is not the idea at all. He points out first that breath control, as developed to its physical ultimate as we find it in hibernating animals, conserves energy and longevity but does not itself conduce to spiritual enlightenment except in so far as it represents a conquest by the adept of his lower self. Breath-control is therefore just a way of asserting one's mental control over one's own body. It has however a less negative side. Tibetan yogis apparently believed that there is a connection between thinking and breathing: the sequence or movement of one's thinking changes as the rate of one's breathing changes. The duration of a thought similarly changes with the duration of breath. Breath-control thus trains the mind to function independently of the bodily process of breathing.

Things seem more than a little awry here. Obviously different people believe different things and nothing can be done about it. In just the same way, we saw with the martial artists that one cannot really get agreement on what people even think they mean by such fundamental terms as 'breath-power' or 'circular movement'. It is perhaps possible to suggest one way out of the problem, by looking at what actually seems to be happening, rather than at the terms that people use to describe things. On this basis one could say simply that, first of all, the disposition of body and mind involved in the process of correct breathing is conducive to the development of intrinsic energy; and secondly, one of the most effective ways in which the development of intrinsic energy can be gauged is through the amount of mental control the adept can exert over his own involuntary bodily processes, like breathing. Breathing is thus both a means of acquiring occult powers, and a way of proving that one has acquired them.

What of course always remains to be shown is that such occult powers are really there to be acquired in the first place. We have already noted the staggering list of powers compiled by Patanjali. The difficulty is to find out how many of these have really been cultivated by yogis. It is not merely a case here of piercing through a wall of xenophobia and suspicion, such as that erected by the Chinese to prevent full comprehension of internal boxing from reaching the detested world outside. The problem here is rather that the genuine yogi claims to regard any occult powers that might accrue to him as being positive obstacles on the path to true enlightenment, because of the temptations which they raise of seeking temporal satisfactions and glory, rather than eternal bliss. He is therefore likely to be most unwilling to demonstrate them, for fear of thereby straying from the true way, in a manner which may well set back his progress to enlightenment through several incarnations. At best, he will regard them, in the words of Swami Chidananda, as merely 'ripe fruit that has come to the tree after it has grown for eight, ten, or twelve years'. In any event, genuine yogis also adhere to a law of silence, which requires them to disclose secrets only to disciples who have obtained the necessary qualifications.

A yogi can thus plead legitimately that there are very serious considerations inhibiting him from making any public demonstration of any occult powers that he might have developed. It is nonetheless rather disconcerting to find Sri Aurobindo referring to a 'discovery or an extension of these little-known or yet undeveloped powers [of occultism]'[1] as if he did not know of any that had been developed already, especially in view of his own readiness to claim to have had a personal vision of Lord Krishna sitting beside him on the bench in the magistrate's court in which Aurobindo was facing trial for conspiring to overthrow the British Government.

All this of course implies that any yogi who does consent to perform in public is very likely to be, in the words of Australian yogi Swami Karunanda, a yogi who is not absolutely pure in his spiritual life, and could therefore be described as neurotic. Other Swamis have denounced so-called yogis who can drink nitric acid, swallow nails, bend iron bars with their hands and allow steam rollers to pass over their chests. Such yogis, we may presume, are not likely to have advanced far along the path of enlightenment. We could therefore take it that they would not have developed occult powers to a very high degree, and would thus be uncommonly likely to fail disastrously when they attempted to do anything out of the ordinary in public. On the other hand, there is no doubt that nothing would be more likely to persuade the sceptic of the essential validity of yoga teaching, than a really convincing demonstration of acid-drinking, nail-swallowing and so on. The trouble is that even the most genuine of yogis might well be unable to mobilize sufficient intrinsic energy in the required manner, at the required time, for such a performance, for any number of reasons which would seemingly reflect no discredit on his spiritual state. His physical energy might be below par; he might be unable to achieve the requisite degree of mental concentration, or detachment, whichever was required; or there might be all manner of unsympathetic vibrations in the atmosphere which might make it impossible for him to get going. What is regrettably the case is that there have been any number of attempts by yogis, genuine or neurotic, to display their occult gifts in public, which have resulted in the most ghastly fiascos.

One might quote for example the experience of Lakshamanasandra Srikanta Rao, who according to Milbourne Christopher was a hatha-yogi who had previously eaten nails, needles, razor blades and glass, and had therefore done everything which the raja-yogis say that he should not have done. Rao attempted to walk on water in India in 1966. An oblong concrete tank twenty feet long and six feet wide had been built for the occasion. The yogi ascended the steps to the side of the tank; paused in prayer; stepped confidently on to the surface of the water; and immediately sank to the bottom.

It might charitably be said that this kind of thing could well happen to anybody. Quite different language has to be used to describe the cases where yogis, who are obviously very far from absolutely pure in their spiritual lives, have deliberately tried to deceive their gullible audiences. The most blatant examples of this have naturally been in the most spectacular fields of occult performance: burial alive, and levitation. Andrija Puharich reports in his book *Beyond Telepathy* (Longmans, London, 1962) that yogis and fakirs have publicly performed by being buried alive for as long as thirty days. At the end of this period, the yogi, although understandably dehydrated, and having lost weight, has been found to be in good health.[7]

But the sad case is that there is no convincingly attested evidence that anything of the kind has ever been done. There is on the other hand abundant evidence of the most extraordinary kinds of deception which various 'neurotic' yogis have resorted to. In the first place, one might mention that nobody has ever been buried alive in full public view for days, or even for hours. Most audiences are in fact quite satisfied with demonstrations lasting up to ten or twelve minutes. These indeed would be remarkable enough if it meant that the yogi had held his breath for this period. But nothing of the kind is involved: J. B. S. Haldane has proved that there is sufficient oxygen in even an airtight container with a capacity of two and a half cubic feet to sustain a man for an hour, so long as he remained motionless. Feats of burial underground for hours or days are all too easily explained. The liar concerned simply arranges to have an underground tunnel dug beforehand linking his coffin with a place of shelter; he pushes open a flap in the coffin after burial and crawls away to safety; and returns in excellent physical condition at a convenient time before being triumphantly dug up. One can simply put burial alive away with water dowsing: there is no reason to believe that either have ever been performed in such a way as to demonstrate occult powers.

However, there can be no denying that there is super-abundant testimony of variously impressive kinds, that at least some yogis are occasionally willing and able to perform feats as incompatible with the laws of physics and anatomy as those performed so often and regularly by the internal boxers. No less an authority than Professor Basham has declared in his book *The Wonder that was India* that:

The awakened *kundalini* gives to the yogi superhuman power and knowledge, and many yogis have practised yoga for this rather than for salvation. Some adepts of yoga have developed powers which cannot be fully accounted for by European medical science, and which cannot be explained away as subjective ...

Professor Basham then goes on rather surprisingly to assert unequivocally that 'the physiological basis of laya- and hatha-yoga is certainly false, there is no *kundalini*.' This naturally raises the question of what it is that when awakened gives the yogi these superhuman powers, especially as Professor Basham then continues:

... whatever we may think about his spiritual claims, there is no doubt that the advanced yogi can hold his breath for very long periods without suffering injury, can control the rhythm of his own heartbeats, can withstand extremes of heat and cold, can remain healthy on a starvation diet, and, despite his austere and frugal life, and his remarkable physical contortions, which would ruin the system of any ordinary man, can often survive to a very advanced age with full use of his faculties.[8]

This catalogue of achievement would be impressive enough by any standards. It also most fortunately includes a number of activities which it has been possible to test scientifically. The combined result of these experiments, conducted at widely separated institutions, has been the very worst that sceptics might have feared: the physically impossible has been done, and it seems as if it can probably be done by almost anybody with the right disposition.

It must be admitted at the outset that the records of these experiments do not necessarily make very exciting reading. There is no doubt that the atmosphere of scientific or medical institutions is uniquely unsympathetic to displays of occult phenomena. This might of course be because they are uniquely unfavourable for the perpetration of frauds. But it is also true that even the possessor of genuinely occult powers might be inhibited in any number of ways from producing them to their best effect in scientifically controlled conditions. The Japanese and Chinese masters recognize that there are days on which the *ki* is flowing more satisfactorily than on other days. It is fair to assume that only the masters themselves can perform to order, regardless of place or time and they of course are least likely to risk their reputations in this way.

The fact remains that tests have been made in conditions which preclude any possibility of fraud and these tests have revealed that some yogis at least possess powers of control over their involuntary bodily processes which are not satisfactorily explained, to put it at the mildest. In 1962 three Indian doctors, M. A. Wenger, B. K. Bagchi and B. K. Anand carried out experiments in breath-control with four yogis. The first two were able to restrict their breathing with evidently great muscular tension, involving what seemed to be a compression of the thorax to slow down the circulation of the blood. Their pulse-rates were enfeebled, and the action of their hearts was limited to such an extent that the sound of heart-beats could not be detected, although electro-cardiographs showed that their hearts were in fact still beating. The third yogi, who was presumably having an off day, merely demonstrated how he could control these processes, without actually doing it. But the fourth held his breath while lying on his back and applying a chin-lock on himself, in such a way as to induce a marked slowing of heartbeats and respiration. The doctors conducting the experiment could only conclude that he had managed in some unknown way first to stimulate and then to interrupt the action of the vagus nerve.[9]

There was nothing very spectacular about this, as has been said, although the inexplicable, however dull, cannot help but be impressive. But an experiment carried out in 1970 at the All-India Institute, Delhi, was considerably more remarkable. A yogi was placed in an airtight metal container screwed and clamped shut. The yogi then went into a self-induced trance. He admittedly rang the alarm bell in a disappointingly short time of about three-quarters of an hour, showing some signs of distress. However, it was discovered that he had in that time not only slowed the rate of his heart-beats considerably, but had actually consumed only one-quarter of the normal minimum requirement of oxygen, and without applying any of the muscular contortions used by the participants in the 1962 experiments.

This demonstration at the All-India Institute fulfilled exactly the requirements of the process detailed by Andrija Puharich in his description of breath-control or *Pranayama*, in which the adept exerts mental control over his respiration with the object of slowing down normal respiratory rhythm, or even stopping it altogether for periods. The ultimate goal is supposed to be rather unflatteringly that of the state of slow respiration developed by hibernating animals. But even more remarkable was the parallel experiment conducted by Professor Neil Miller at the Rockefeller University, New York, in which a subject not trained in yoga techniques was requested to control his respiration and heart action by simply deciding to do so. Electro-cardiographs were set up to a graph on the wall. The subject was instructed by Professor Miller to try to cause the graph to fall by slowing down the rate of his involuntary bodily processes. He did so. More than that, it was also discovered at the Rockefeller Institute that animals can similarly be trained to modify their internal functions on demand.

At this point, one needs to stop and think. It is perhaps not surprising that persons trained in the extraordinary contortions of hatha-yoga should be able to compress or distend their muscles in such a way as to affect the flow of blood to their internal organs, and thus exercise some control over the respiratory and pulse-rates. But it is quite astonishing that raja-yogis can produce the same results without any apparent contortions, and still more remarkable that westerners, untrained in yoga at all, can control their autonomic nervous systems by the mere exercise of the will.

One is again reminded of the situation in the martial arts, where it seems possible to develop intrinsic energy in so many different ways, that it could be argued that one might develop it in any way at all, given only the determination to do so. But it is not only untrained westerners who appear to be able to achieve feats of mind over matter which are at least comparable with those of the great yogis. There is reason enough to believe that occult powers are not even confined to human beings. The long migratory travels of fish and birds through and over uncharted seas are really not explicable in any material terms.[10] More than that, tests made in France by Pierre Duval and E. Montredon to gauge the capacity of mice to avoid electric shocks by detecting by precognition the particular part of the test area in which the shock would next occur, indicated convincingly that the mice knew where to jump. Mice like men can beat chance with occult powers of perception. However, there are some differences: as far as is known, no mouse, fish or bird has yet been able to raise itself off the ground and hover in the air without the use of wings, or cause objects to move by the exercise of mental power alone. Men can.

Tibetan yoga

Tibetan yoga has obvious parallels with Indian yoga. It is based on the same philosophical concepts, makes the same claim to occult powers, and utilizes the same physical exercises in order to acquire these powers. The main technical difference is possibly in an emphasis on yantra- or mantra-yoga, involving the employment of geometrical diagrams with occult significance or the repetition of certain phrases in order to bring about desired changes in the physical universe. Tibetan yoga is thus more easily recognized as a counterpart of European magic: it deals with caballistic signs and formulas; it draws circles and uses incantations. But there is another more significant difference for students of the occult. The difference is one of style. Indian yoga is primarily concerned with great human problems. It is bewilderingly modest in its occult pretensions. The Tibetans are at once more esoteric and more boastful. The undeniable impression for a westerner at least is one of comparative vulgarity.

One effect of this is certainly to make the analysis of Tibetan yoga rather fruitless for our purpose. There is no end to the pretensions of the Tibetans. The problem is rather to produce any incontrovertible evidence that the pretensions are founded at all on fact. It seems uncommonly difficult to find a Tibetan yogi who has some first-hand acquaintance of the powers which Tibetan yogis unhesitatingly claim to possess.

This was the problem facing Dr Alfonso Caycedo, when he widened his investigations from Indian to Tibetan yoga. The Dalai Lama should certainly be the man best qualified to explain what his followers were capable of. He assured Dr Caycedo in fact that adepts of Tibetan yoga could see objects millions of miles away as clearly as if they were right in front of them; they could see beyond death; they could hear the divine sound (presumably the 'continuous vibrant inner quasi-sound' referred to by Rosalind Heywood as 'the Singing'); they can read minds; they can levitate by drawing their breath and controlling it; they can disintegrate their bodies when they know that they are going to die; and they can fall gradually without getting hurt. More than that, a Tibetan yogi in the state of *domo* or transcendental wisdom can radiate beams of light from his body; he can stand in the sun without casting a shadow; he can make his body vanish; he can transform stones into gold and walk upon water without sinking; he can enter into fire without being burned; he can melt a snow-mountain; he can travel to a far-off cosmos in a few seconds; he can fly in the sky; and he can walk through rocks and mountains. The only difficulty is to find a Tibetan yogi who has actually done some of these things, or who is prepared to say that he has seen any other Tibetan yogi do them.

This is not so easy. The Dalai Lama apparently could not or would not demonstrate these powers. His advisers were not much more help. One of them claimed to have seen the process of disintegrating the body before death, at least in its earlier stages: he had entered the cell where another monk had died, and he thought that the corpse of the monk was noticeably smaller than his living body had been. Another said that he had heard that another monk called Tinley could levitate, although he had never actually seen him do it. Dr Caycedo was able to obtain a photograph of the English-sounding but by no means English-looking Tinley, but unfortunately no more convincing evidence that Tinley could leviate.

There is indeed no documentary evidence that Tibetan yogis can do anything out of the ordinary. There is however a considerable body of myth and travellers' tales, more or less convincing. There is for example the biography of *Tibet's Great Yogi Milrepa*, by E. Y. Evans-Wentz. Milrepa flourished in the eleventh century AD, after the monk Alisha had come to Tibet from India in 1038, to reform and revitalize the flagging Tibetan priesthood. As portrayed by Dr Evans-Wentz, Milrepa certainly emerges as one of the truly noble minds of humanity. He is also supposed to have developed his psychic nerve-centres to such effect that he could levitate at will; fly through the air with the speed of an arrow; and sustain life by osmosis, without having to go through the mundane bodily processes of ingestion, digestion and excretion.

One has here the usual double problem. In the first place, one might feel that a man of the quality of Milrepa, like indeed a man of the quality of Mahomet or Christ for that matter, would be inclined to tell the truth himself, and would inspire his biographers to be similarly scrupulous. On the other hand, legends do grow regardless of the wishes of the people concerned, and one really feels the need of some concrete evidence for occult powers nearer in time than the eleventh century.

There are of course contemporary witnesses, at least one of whom has been described as inspiring immediate confidence. Julian Duguid, reviewing Alexandra David-Neil's book, *Magic and Mystery in Tibet* for the Society for Psychical Research, described the book as 'remarkably honest'. He had no doubts at all that Miss David-Neil was describing events that had really happened to her. Mr Duguid, as an adventurer and explorer himself, should certainly be as competent as anybody at recognizing a true story when he hears one. In this case, as so often happens, it is easy to find adequate corroboration. The part of Miss David-Neil's book to which he was particularly referring, was that in which she described how she succeeded by intense and sustained concentration in materializing the form of a Tibetan monk to keep her company in her solitude. The monk however developed a personality of his own, quite unlike what she had intended him to possess, and one which she found increasingly quarrelsome and disagreeable. It became necessary after a while for her to try to dematerialize him. The monk resisted vigorously, but eventually was made to vanish.[11]

It is certainly difficult to imagine exactly what is going on here. There is however parallel testimony of the most convincing kind. Dr G. H. Estabrooks describes how he himself managed to hallucinate a pet polar bear for his entertainment. The bear would parade around the hospital and jump out of windows on response to mental commands from Dr Estabrooks. However, the bear began to turn up in unexpected places, and without being summoned into existence by the count of five which Dr Estabrooks used for his experiment in auto-suggestion. Dr Estabrooks accordingly found it necessary to banish the bear and tell him never to return. Apparently the bear obeyed without resistance, unlike Miss David-Neil's Tibetan monk.

One may of course only be witnessing in both these cases nothing more than a combination of self-induced hallucination, plus the kind of experience known to every creative writer, in which a 'made-up' character takes on a personality and style of speech and behaviour of its own, which may well seem to be quite independent of the will of its creator. It is certainly in the same category of experience as the 'God realization' of the Indian yogis. One must recall that Dr Paul Brunton has argued that the common belief that ideas are only to be seen within one's head, so to speak, is a false belief, and that external reality is itself perceived just as much within the head as creations of the imagination are. At the same time, one must admit some difference between visions which can be seen only by the person imagining them, whether he sees them inside his head or outside it, and objectively 'real' things which are visible to others as well. The subjective and the objective may well both be real, but their reality must be in different dimensions.[12] Certainly, no one else saw Dr Estabrooks's bear, and Miss David-Neil does not suggest that anybody else actually saw her monk.

Miss David-Neil has, however, recorded some experiences which would have to be called objective. One of the most remarkable was her meeting with a *lung-gom-pa* lama. This monk passed her in the mountains, travelling at terrific speed by a continuous series of bounds, rather than normal running. She discovered later that the lama must have kept this up nonstop for at least a couple of days. It was explained to her that Tibetan yogis can acquire this skill by a combination of quiet sitting and breath-control until they cease to become aware of the weight and mass of their own bodies. That this is an objective rather than purely subjective phenomenon is attested by the fact that they have to gird themselves with chains to keep in reasonable contact with the earth.

Such a capacity for rapid and effortless locomotion would undoubtedly be particularly useful in Tibet: as Dr Evans-Wentz points out, Milrepa's capacity to fly through the air like an arrow meant that he had no need of modern technology: in particular, he would not have needed an automobile. Possibly even more useful in that part of the world would be the ability to withstand or counteract cold. This is another power of the Tibetans to which Miss David-Neil and Dr Paul Brunton have both testified. Miss David-Neil explains how she has seen hermits in the Tibetan mountains existing in the freezing winter, protected, or rather not protected by one thin garment. On other occasions, she has seen neophytes wrapped in wet and ice-cold sheets sitting calmly in the winter snow in the Himalayas. Here again we have physical matter not reacting naturally to physical conditions. Again too we have a startlingly detailed formula for achieving this particular phenomenon of mind over matter. One adopts a meditative posture; exerts breath-control by depressing the chest and shoulders, expanding the abdomen and slowing the rate of respiration; and visualizes suns in one's hands and feet. When these have been materialized or auto-suggested into existence with sufficient conviction, one rubs one's hands and feet until the suns burst into flame. One then concludes the ritual with 'twenty-one big leaps', which will doubtless help to keep one warm for a time at least, even if the materialized suns have not succeeded in doing so.

It is scarcely necessary to say that nobody has been prepared to swear that he has actually witnessed this spectacular exercise of a Tibetan yogi's *domo*. What we are left with is a collection of anecdotes, to all impressions both serious and honest, testifying to the Tibetans' powers of telepathy, ('sending messages on the wind'); their extraordinary and apparently superhuman physical endurance as long-distance runners; and their quite superhuman talent for not being affected by cold or heat. We do after all need only one superhuman feat of this kind to prove that mind over matter is a reality. The world still awaits the first Tibetan yogi who will present himself at the All-India Institute; allow himself to be shut up in a refrigerator under laboratory conditions; and successfully defy the cold through the exercise of his *domo*.

6 Mind over matter:
levitation, telekinesis

Levitation

Beyond any question at all, the most spectacular demonstration
of the powers of mind over matter which any number of people
have actually claimed to experience, is that of levitation.
Nobody has ever actually seen anything more surprising than a
human body or other solid object floating in the air. It is also
the kind of phenomenon which carries with it a peculiar quality
of conviction: it might be possible to explain away the occult
feats of the martial artists by assuming that a million or so
people of every imaginable diversity are involved in a conspiracy of no very clear advantage to any of them; but one
cannot conspire with the force of gravity. Levitation beats
everything.

That being so, it is not surprising that levitation and telekinesis have both attracted some of the most industrious fakers.
The crudest technique is undoubtedly that of phoney or neurotic yogis who allowed themselves to be photographed, apparently floating in the air, swathed in their robes, with one arm
extended and the hand resting lightly on a stick thrust into the
ground, and also swathed in cloth. It was all too easy for sceptics to point out that the cloth-covered stick was really a metal
post firmly embedded in the ground, which was shaped at the
top to form a frame in which the yogi sat securely, his deception concealed by his flowing robes.

An even simpler technique for indoor levitation in darkened
rooms has been explained by Mr Christopher. The levitator
wears a pair of loose-fitting shoes. He arranges for two of his

audience to place their hands under his shoes while he sits between them in a darkened room. He then slips his feet out of the
shoes, put his hands in the shoes instead, and gradually raises
them, thus giving his two victims the impression that he is
rising bodily off the ground. All one needs for successful deception in this way is total darkness, moderate dexterity and
half-witted and preferably blind assistants.

But the fact is that one has more than sufficient testimony to
the fact that this most remarkable of occult phenomena has
really happened, from witnesses who are at least not likely to
have been either half-witted or blind. For example, Ernest
Wood remarks matter-of-factly in his book, *Yoga* (Cassell,
London, 1962), that:

Levitation or rising of a body from the ground and its suspension
a few feet up in the air above the seat or couch is a universally
accepted fact in India. I remember one occasion when an old
yogi was levitated in a recumbent posture about six feet above the
ground in an open field for about one and a half hours, while the
visitors were permitted to pass sticks to and fro in the space
between.

He also quotes the testimony of Princess Pana Choki, the
second daughter of the Maharajah of Sikkim, concerning her
uncle, whom she describes for excellent reason as

the most extraordinary man I've ever met. I remember that when
I was a little girl he ... did what you would call exercises in
levitation. I used to take him a little rice. He would be motionless
in mid-air. Every day he rose a little higher. In the end he rose so
high that I found it difficult to hand the rice up to him. I was a
little girl, and I had to stand on tiptoe ... There are certain
things you don't forget.[1]

There are indeed, and handing up rice to an uncle floating in
mid-air would rank high among them. The importance of these
testimonies is of course two-fold. In the first place, the possibility of fakery scarcely exists. Wood recounts how witnesses
were allowed to pass sticks underneath the yogi to ensure that
he could not be supported in any way from underneath, and

there certainly could be no question of his being supported from above. Similarly, the princess must have noticed during her visits to replenish her uncle, if there was in fact anything that could have been holding him up. In the second place, the eminence of the witnesses can only be regarded as tending to guarantee their honesty. Prominent people are less likely to tell lies in cases like this than obscure people, because there would be more people to laugh at them if they were found out.

This factor applies perhaps most significantly in the case of Dr V. M. Bhat whose own credentials as former revolutionary, doctor and scientist undoubtedly command respect. What is still more impressive, however, is the fact that his book has been commended by a former Governor of Bihar Province, Mr M. S. Aney; by Dr R. D. Ranade, Professor of Philosophy at Allahabad University; by the ex-Governor of Bombay, Hare Krishna Mehtab; and by his Chief Minister, Mr B. G. Kher. High officials and academics are as prone to self-delusion as anybody else, though they may be a little more difficult to gull than most; but they are certainly among the least likely people publicly to associate themselves with something liable to make them look ridiculous. One can only presume that they at least believed that Dr Bhat has seen what he says he has seen, and that nobody is likely to be able to prove differently.

Unfortunately, Dr Bhat has not himself apparently witnessed a case of levitation. However, he reports that his colleague Dr Limaye once saw another friend of his, Purohit Swami, rise off the ground while meditating, and remain suspended there for a time; and that the Swami himself had once described how he had seen another yogi perform the same feat. Another friend of Dr Bhat's, a Mr Nirokhekar, had seen the yogi Budbudacharya levitating himself and passing through a solid wall.[2]

Second- and third-hand reports of this kind can never be very satisfactory. However, the fact is, as E. J. Harrison says, that levitation is widely accepted in the East as a reality, even though there is nothing more difficult than to find somebody who claims to have seen it done, let alone anyone who claims to

be able to do it. This general acceptance is indeed not surprising, when one remembers how thoroughly the phenomenon
has been documented even outside Asia. One naturally tends to
disbelieve anything unusual that was supposed to have happened more than ten years ago, but it must be admitted that the
flights of St Joseph of Cupertino in the twelfth century seem to
have been as well attested to as any events in history.

Almost the same could be said of the levitations of the Vic-
torian medium, Daniel Douglas Home. Admittedly, Milbourne
Christopher casts every possible doubt on Home's apparent
levitation at Ashley House, where he was supposed to have
floated out of one window and come in at another; but the Ashley
House performance was only one out of literally over a hundred
instances where Home seems to have risen from the ground in
the presence of witnesses of considerable social prominence and
presumed reliability. These witnesses have also attested that
Home performed his feats in broad daylight, to make it evident
that no fraud was involved. Dr Estabrooks suggests that he
would himself seemingly duplicate everything Home did, by
simply getting hold of a number of good hypnotic subjects;
persuading them that they had seen him floating through the
air, objects rising from the ground, and so on; and obtaining
their sworn affidavits to this effect while they were still under
hypnosis. It would have involved a colossal fraud, as he says, of
a size which at the very least would be hardly worth the trouble
and risk. No other technique could explain in material terms
Home's capacity to levitate himself and solid objects, in full
light, in rooms which he had not entered beforehand.

In any event, it would be a little difficult for even an immensely competent hypnotist to mesmerize witnesses on the
first floor of a building to make them think that he had left via
the window, then run upstairs to the sixth floor, and mesmerize
a further group into thinking that he had come in through a
window. It all seems so unnecessary. Besides, there is always
the fact that hypnotism itself, as we have seen, can perform
feats which there is no material explanation, so that hypnotism also has to be regarded as an occult power.

The difficulty with Home of course is that sceptics are compelled to assume that everything he did had to be fraudulent, simply because nothing that he did was ever proved to be fraudulent. It is not too hard to discredit in this way a man long safely dead. It is however a different matter entirely to discredit prominent living men who make claims every bit as remarkable as Home's. The most formidable of these claimants is undoubtedly the Jesuit, Father Oscar Gonzalez-Quevado, director of the Latin American Centre of Parapsychology, São Paulo, Brazil. Fr Gonzalez-Quevado's two major works, *A Face Oculta da Mente*, and *As Forças Fisicas da Mente*, (Edicões Loyola, São Paulo) have been described by North American, Latin and European experts as quite simply by far the best, most comprehensive, most impartial and most fully-documented studies in the field of parapsychology and the occult ever written. Among his other achievements, some of which will be referred to later, Fr Gonzalez-Quevado has, for the benefit of the Brazilian press, performed feats of levitating subjects in broad daylight, out-of-doors, in the presence of witnesses who were allowed to pass hoops over the bodies of the subjects, to make sure that there was no solid but invisible means of support either above or below them. Some situations can be stated simply. Fr Gonzalez-Quevado is either a liar with hypnotic powers, or a levitator. If he can levitate, there is no reason why Dr Bhat's yogi friends might not have levitated too.

It is appropriate to pause at this point and try to decide just what levitation would actually involve, technically speaking, if indeed there were any such phenomenon. It is clearly not just a case of one's becoming unconscious of the weight of one's own body, as the Tibetans explained to Miss David-Neil. It is not consciousness that holds one down, but gravity, and gravity is presumably not conscious of anything. Levitation can only mean that some force is being operated in a quasi-magnetic manner, which is strong enough to counter gravitational pull. One has to say quasi-magnetic here, because it clearly operates, if it operates at all, without anything like sufficient electrical force being generated, and without any question of the appropriate magnetic poles being opposed. It also works as gravity does, with substances which have no magnetic properties. In other words, the resemblance to magnetism as understood in physical science, is limited to the ability of the force employed to repel or attract objects at a distance.

Telekinesis

Levitation is thus fundamentally a variety of telekinesis, the ability to influence objects at a distance by the exercise of the will, listed by Patanjali among the gifts of yoga. It is also the particular manifestation of the influence of mind over matter with which students of the occult and parapsychology have always had the most trouble, partly because it is the hardest of all to believe in or to understand, but also because it is the easiest and most impressive to fake. Probably more frauds have been exposed in the area of telekinesis or levitation than in any other areas of the occult. Favourite techniques for deception have included the use of magnets concealed on the person of the fake medium; cotton threads attached beforehand to objects which the medium will pretend to attract by occult powers; and most elaborately, telescopic metal rods concealed up the sleeves of the medium, which are extruded as required under cover of darkness. Bundles of silk or cheesecloth are sometimes stored in this way and extruded along with the metal rods to conceal their operation. The material thus pushed out is of course described by the medium as 'ectoplasm', produced by the exteriorization of occult forces. On the other hand, there are limits to what can be done with metal rods and cheesecloth. Home for example somehow materialized hands in semi-darkness at a distance of nine or ten feet, which were able to pick up flowers from under the nose of one of the women present, and place them on her head. This might have been the real thing, or it might have been hypnotism, but it could hardly have been metal rods.

The fact is that one cannot be deterred from serious investigation of a subject, simply because of frauds which are known or suspected to have taken place. Levitation and telekinesis are in themselves no more unaccountable than the use of the *ch'i* in the martial arts to produce physical effects without physical causes; their validity has been attested to in modern times by witnesses who can only be described as impressively reliable; and the existence of telekinesis as a force has been repeatedly demonstrated in some of the dreariest and most laborious of scientific experiments, which should by now have convinced anybody who was not determined not to be convinced.

It must at the same time be admitted that the earlier attempts by Rhine and his followers at Duke University, Carolina, were uniquely unsatisfactory. This was at least partly due to the primitive nature of the equipment used in the first experiments. A table was designed with a blanketed top and a fixed retaining wall. The subject would attempt to influence dice to fall into a target area when a frictionless barrier was raised, allowing them to roll down a slope on to the table. Virtually all that these tests proved was that very few dice are manufactured without a bias. However, tests of what is either telekinesis or perhaps precognition have since been carried out successfully at the highest level of sophistication by physicist Helmut Schmidt, who allows subjects to predict events on the theoretically unpredictable quantum level initiated by radioactive decay. Schmidt uses electronic apparatus with completely automated recording devices, thus eliminating all possibility of human error. Fellow-physicists, who may well be the only people who fully understand what Schmidt is doing, are deeply impressed.

But there are again convincing testimonials of a perhaps slightly less sophisticated though not necessarily less reliable kind. Dr Bhat tells how he saw a Muslim fakir make a rupee coin jump into his hands from a distance of ten feet. Paul Brunton similarly claims to have met a fakir who could make a coin, loaned to him by Brunton for the purpose, dance along a table; make a ring of Brunton's rise and fall in the air at command; and levitate a small iron bar and a steel-handled knife.

More recently, and perhaps more authoritatively, Dr Ricardo Musso, President of the Argentine Society of Parapsychology, and Director of Parapsychology at the University of the Littoral, in Rosario, Argentina, testified in 1961 that he had witnessed his first display of levitation or telekinesis. Under the best possible conditions for observation, the subject raised a small table weighing about twenty-five pounds, a foot and a half off the ground, without physical contact, and kept it there while Dr Musso and his colleague, Dr Butelman, Professor of Social Psychology and of the History of Psychology at the National University of Buenos Aires, made all the observations that they wanted to. More than that, the two professors were actually able to sit on the table while it was being held in the air by telekinesis.

Dr Musso was of course a friend of Fr Gonzalez-Quevado's. The sceptic can therefore suggest that the three Latin Americans conspired with a phoney medium to cook up a tissue of lies for reasons which can only be imagined. There is indeed nothing else that the sceptic can suggest.

Some other explanation would, however, have to be found to account for the submissions of Soviet biologist Edward Naumov on his tests with Nelya Mikhailova, former senior sergeant of the 226th Tank Regiment, heroine of the siege of Leningrad, wife of an engineer, mother of a Red Army cadet, and in general ideal citizeness of the Soviet Union. Mrs Mikhailova apparently made compass needles spin, matches move across a table and fall off it, and attracted cigarettes, a piece of bread and the white of a raw egg, among other totally non-magnetic objects. Most of the objects affected in these tests were enclosed in non-magnetic metal cases or plexiglass containers or both, to eliminate any possibility that Mrs Mikhailova might have had magnets or other electronic aids concealed on her person, or might have been using invisible wire to influence the objects being tested. It would of course be difficult to imagine any magnet or mechanical aid that could work on the white of an egg. One might hesitate to say that telekinesis is a fact, in the words of Fr Gonzalez-Quevado, simply because it would be the most extraordinary fact that the human mind has ever had to take account of. The trouble is that it is becoming really too difficult to say anything else.

The whole question of telekinesis received quite startling publicity during the second half of 1973, from the performances of Mr Uri Geller, a twenty-six-year-old Israeli living in London. Telekinesis is, of course, impossible according to the accepted laws of physical science and, being impossible, is necessarily incredible; and one can hardly talk sensibly of anything being more incredible and impossible than anything else. However, there is no doubt that Mr Geller's demonstrations, if they were genuine, would be by far the most important demonstrations of the impossible and incredible in recorded history, simply because they were so widely observed and rigorously scrutinized, and because they indicate even more than the feats of Mrs Mikhailova that the operations of occult forces simply cannot be reconciled with the logic of the physical universe.

Mr Geller first attracted attention when he appeared on a radio show hosted by Jimmy Young, at which he bent or broke keys and paper-knives held by Mr Young, by gently stroking them. What was really remarkable, however, was that spoons and forks owned by people listening to the programme all over England also apparently broke or became distorted. The same thing happened when Mr Geller appeared on television. Cutlery bent, tools snapped and watches stopped. It was, of course, still just barely believable by those who would prefer to believe in anything except the occult, that another gigantic hoax was in operation. This explanation was rendered rather more incredible by the fact that a Cambridge physicist challenged Mr Geller to break a number of steel screwdrivers inside a metal box without touching them. The box was opened; the screwdrivers were found to be broken; and the Department of Metallurgy at Cambridge professed itself unable to explain how the fractures of the tools could be duplicated.

Mr Geller then naturally visited the United States. He allowed himself to be subjected to tests under laboratory conditions at the Stanford Institute, California, where he bent metal objects and performed feats of telepathy under the surveillance of American scientists. Once again, the experts could provide no physical explanation for what they had witnessed. They were thereupon ridiculed in their turn by American stage magicians, who claimed that there was nothing easier to delude than an academic expert. Here the professionals were perhaps playing a little out of their league. In the first place, a stage magician may be trained in deluding an audience anxious to be hocussed. He is not professionally equipped to carry out scientific experiments or to evaluate evidence. Moreover, it would not necessarily prove Mr Geller fraudulent if a hundred stage magicians were able to duplicate his feats through trickery. It would still have to be proved that he was using tricks too. In any case, no stage magician has attempted to do what Mr Geller was doing at Stanford, under the same laboratory conditions. The show business critics simply did not have a case. It is, moreover, worth noting that there was a professional magician on the testing team at Stanford. He could not explain Mr Geller's powers either.

The antipathy of stage magicians is not difficult to understand. It is simply the natural reaction of any industrial organization to competition from non-union labour. It was perhaps more than usually uncalled-for in this case, because Mr Geller's own performances under show business conditions were not wholly successful. He failed completely to bend nails on Johnny Carson's late night television show. Mr Geller complained that the atmosphere was unsympathetic, as indeed it well might have been. He also at first failed to bend metal objects on stage in New York, although he was moderately successful with telepathy. Here again he explained that he was too tense and concentrating too much. However, he then asked some of the women in the audience to bring rings on stage, and apparently recovered his telekinetic gifts in this more relaxed and congenial company.

Obviously, one can hardly come to a final judgement about Mr Geller on the evidence available. There is nonetheless no

doubt at all about where the balance of probability lies. The
Stanford tests at least can only have been genuine, and certainly satisfied the testers. The fork-bending on British radio
and television was hardly scientifically controlled, and some of
the technicians on the set on one occasion at least believed that
Mr Geller was using force to bend the objects concerned.
Others were convinced he did not. There is some difficulty
here. It does not require exceptional physical strength to bend a
spoon or fork, although even a very strong man could hardly
conceal the fact that muscular strength was being used. However, only a professional strong man, which Mr Geller obviously is not, could possibly bend keys with his fingers, and
nobody watching him could have any doubt that he was using
more than mental energy to do it. Breaking unbreakable metal
screwdrivers in a closed box without touching them is something else again.

So are the phenomena of long-range telekinesis which are
supposed to have taken place during Mr Geller's shows. Here
indeed one may postulate a gigantic conspiracy including the
BBC, Jimmy Young and David Dimbleby, who held latchkeys
for Mr Geller to bend. All one can ask is why people who live
by their reputations for credibility could possibly become involved in such a hoax, especially when they would certainly be
paid more by any Sunday newspaper for revealing the hoax
than they possibly could be by Mr Geller for taking part in it.
Even Mr Geller does not have that kind of money. There are
things harder to believe than telekinesis.

There are three final comments to be made on the Geller
phenomenon. The first and simplest is that several people have
apparently been inspired to emulate Mr Geller, including a
seven-year-old boy in Suffolk, Mark Shelley, who claims to
have bent six forks, one after the other. This is not so surprising. Mr Geller is presumably a human being, and it would
be extraordinary if other human beings did not possess the
same faculties as he does. What is a lot more difficult to com-
prehend, however, is the fact that Mr Geller's telekinesis seems
to operate quite differently from that of previously recorded

demonstrations. Telekinesis may be physically impossible, but its manifestations usually make a kind of physical sense. That is to say, telekinetic effects normally appear to be produced by some kind of invisibly projected force, which either shatters immovable objects, or pushes movable ones around. Mr Geller's telekinesis cannot work this way. Either it works as a two-way force, which keeps an object steady by applying pressure in one direction, so that it can be forced out of shape by an opposing pressure applied simultaneously; or else it must produce a molecular change in the object being acted upon, akin to that produced by intense heat, so that a solid object thus becomes soft and pliable. There is no doubt that the second explanation is easier to credit than the first. However, Dr Chilton of the Cambridge University Metallurgy Department insists that there were 'no signs of cutting, burning or the use of acid' in the screwdrivers that he examined. Mr Geller himself says that he does not know how his occult forces operate, or how he came by them. We accordingly seem to be back at our original assumption. Phenomena of mind over matter simply are not subject to any rational limits of nature or technique. Any kind of effect can be produced by any kind of means.

But they have hitherto been subject to limits of effective range. Mrs Mikhailova's hand moved only a few inches above the objects she was influencing while being photographed by Russian television. Father Gonzalez-Quevado stands within a couple of feet of the body he is levitating, with his hands about a foot above the subject. Mr Geller, however, can apparently transmit his telekinetic powers literally as far as radio or television beams can be picked up by a receiver. This indeed is not the first time that the physical force of electricity has allegedly been involved in occult phenomena. The voice on the telephone that has been disconnected, the face on the television set that has been switched off are the classic props of the contemporary story of the supernatural. Brad Steiger in his *Strange Disappearances* (Lancer, New York, 1972) lists the case of the call letters KLEE-TV of Houston, Texas, which appeared on the screen of Mr H. C. Taylor on two occasions, the first three years and the second five years after the letters had ceased to be used by Houston. But nothing as impressive in this line as the Geller phenomena has ever happened before.

The logical significance of all this would seem to be quite clear. If forces which operate in the physical universe can be used to boost the effective range of occult forces, then two things seem to follow. One is that the occult forces must be as 'real' and as tangible as the physical ones. The other is that the physical and psychic universes must in fact co-exist. The old spiritualist notions of psychic effects being produced by 'waves in the ether', and of using radio-telegraphy to communicate with the spirit world, are in fact thoroughly logical attempts to explain the inexplicable. The human condition really is to live in more than one world at a time. Modern technology may help to foster with almost irresistible force the impression that we exist in a single and wholly material universe. The fact is that if the Geller phenomena are genuine, then we and our television sets are existing simultaneously in two universes at the very least.

7 The art of feeling no pain:
fire-walking, self-scarification, acupuncture

Ritualistic self-torture is one of the few features common to both western asceticism and oriental occultism. But a consideration of this parallel serves only to emphasize the differences between the two. Christian ascetics have been concerned precisely to cause themselves pain, either to express their contempt for their own bodies or to distract themselves from their bodily demands. The Asians, on the other hand, are usually concerned just as precisely with not causing themselves pain: self-scarification becomes a means of demonstrating the power of their bodies not to be affected by unfavourable physical conditions.

Fire-walking

The most impressive and in many ways the most unsatisfactory way in which this triumph of the body over pain has been demonstrated, is through the old practice of fire-walking, apparently carried out at one time or another in every inhabited continent of the world. Priestesses of ancient Greece used to walk barefoot through a furnace of hot charcoal in honour of the goddess Artemis, in Cappadocia. Devotees of the goddess Feronia in Italy similarly used to walk barefoot over the embers of a fire of pinewood. In modern times, the ceremony is performed in Japan, in India, in the Philippines, in Fiji, Tahiti, and the West Indies. In every instance, the most obvious purpose of the ritual is to demonstrate the immunity from burning, granted by the deity in whose honour it is being performed, to those whose faith is sufficient to induce them to make the walk.

This is not always done with either success or consistency. The Japanese Shinto ritual perhaps deserves first mention, as an impressive demonstration of how a fire-walk should not be performed. E. J. Harrison once participated in the ceremony performed twice yearly at the Shinto Temple in Tokyo. A bed of pine-logs and charcoal was burned in the courtyard of the temple, and fanned by attendants. However, as the time for the ceremony approached, the attendants began to beat the flames out, until a narrow blackened path had been formed between the flowing banks of charcoal. Piles of salt were then placed at either end of the path, into which the Shinto priests rubbed their feet before dashing over the narrow strip where the fire had been beaten out. They were followed by other devotees, who were first dusted with sacred *gohei* paper by the priests, after similarly rubbing their feet in the salt. Harrison went himself. His experiment in the occult on this occasion was a total failure, as his feet were blistered painfully, but only, as he believed, because he had not taken the precaution to rub enough salt on them beforehand.

Harrison was disgusted both by the apparently fraudulent nature of the Japanese fire-walk, and also by the fact that it was explicitly performed for money. The latter characteristic is true also of the Fijian fire-walk, which ranks as one of the island's tourist attractions. However, the fire-walks here and in other Pacific Islands seem far more formidable affairs. San Francisco surgeon G. M. Fergin reported that the heat from the stones prepared for a fire-walk in Raiatea was sufficient to make coconut palm leaves near the scene burst into flame. The heated stones of porous basalt were not beaten black as in Tokyo, but simply swept with pandanus leaves, presumably to provide a clear surface for walking on. Dr Fergin himself walked across unscathed, and without feeling conscious of the intense heat while actually making the walk.

The two most extraordinary things about the ceremony are that unbelieving and soft-footed Europeans have been able to make the walks on occasion with the same kind of immunity as the devotees, and that the clothing of people taking part never

seems to get burned. Dr Fergin's achievement had been pre-
ceded by a Scotch engineer Hillhouse who had made the Shinto
fire-walk unscathed over a bed of this time glowing charcoal.
Similarly, Reginald Adcock accompanied the fakir Ahmed
Hussain in a fire-walk at the Alexandra Palace in April 1937,
before a crowd of eight thousand. On the other hand, the highly
sympathetic Harrison had no occult protection in his much
milder fire-walk, and an American author, Percival Lowell,
who also attempted a Shinto fire-walk, was hospitalized for
three weeks afterwards.

The most heroic attempt to solve these anomalies was made
by the American Mayne Reid Coe Jr, who concluded that perspiration drops might be able to float on their own vapour, thus
providing a barrier between the body of the performer and the
heat. Mr Coe began by touching red-hot steel bars with his
finger-tips, first cautiously but later with increasing confidence.
He then graduated to licking the red-hot bars with his tongue;
dipped his fingers into molten lead without ill-effects; and
finally performed his own fire-walk of four steps on burning
embers. Milbourne Christopher concluded from this that the
fire-walk was a perfectly natural phenomenon. Requirements
for success were the low thermal conductivity of burning or
burned wood embers, confident and therefore steady walking,
and a maximum of two steps with each foot. Anybody could do it.

This was highly scientific, but perhaps not entirely satisfactory. In the first place, there is the problem that some people do
get burned, and some apparently do not. Even the most
confident of men will normally get his fingers burned if he
touches a red-hot poker. The perspiration shield does not evidently work with everybody. Nor is the ceremony invariably
performed over a distance which can be covered with a mere
four steps. Kuda Bux of Kashmir for example repeatedly performed a fire-walk of twenty feet or more, without burning
either his feet or, still more remarkably, his trousers. And
oriental fire-walks are performed today in conditions which are
very far from meeting the requirements listed above.

The most curious is the Chinese variety of fire-walk. A bed

of charcoal is prepared outside a temple, covering a rectangle some thirty feet long by twenty feet wide, and six inches deep. The charcoal is ignited by having kerosene poured over it, and burning papers thrown on top. Attendants keep the fire alight for about an hour and a half by throwing more kerosene over it. The ceremony begins when a charm paper moistened with blood from the tongue of the celebrant is thrown on to the middle of the burning charcoal. European scholars have observed that the paper does not itself catch alight. When the worshippers are about to make the walk, attendants throw bowls of rice and salt on to the embers. The worshippers walk around the fire a few times, then dash back and forth across it, until the bed has been crossed at least once from each of the four directions. The charm paper, which has remained undamaged through all this, bursts into flames when the celebrant turns away to re-enter the temple.

Some of this smacks disagreeably of fraud. The preliminary walking around could help the worshippers to collect some protective dirt and preferably mud on their feet, and the salt and rice thrown on the embers might certainly tend to cool them. The walk itself is also performed in what might be called a wild scramble, interspersed with leaps and bounds. On the other hand, the behaviour of the charm paper remains inexplicable; the worshippers may run across, but they run across repeatedly; and there is no doubt that those responsible for preparing the bed for the fire-walk do all in their power to make sure that it is in fact as hot as possible.

None of these misgivings apply to the Indian fire-walks, observed and photographed by western scholars. A pit is prepared over twenty feet long, with embers which are undoubtedly as hot as they can get. The Hindu worshippers do not charge across like the Chinese, but progress in a leisurely manner, taking as many as a dozen slow steps. Those who fall over in the pit are severely burned about the body, but worshippers can sink in the embers up to the ankles, without suffering burns. There is nothing much more sensitive or thin-skinned than the human ankle.

Most remarkable of all is of course the formal Fijian fire-walk. A pit is dug and filled with stones and blazing logs. The performers leap on to the stones, dressed in garlands of flowers and leaves, and march around, planting their feet firmly on each stone. Here at least nothing seems to go wrong: the feet and legs of the participants are unburned, and their anklets of leaves show no signs of scorching.

Fire-walking has undoubtedly many unsatisfactory features. One is still forced to accept the fact that in many instances at least the skin and clothing of the participants have resisted the effects of heat in a manner which is not explicable in physical terms. This capacity to resist physical damage is apparently not confined to people of any particular ethnic group, nor even to those who actually believe in the efficacy of the ritual which they participate in. Some people get themselves and their clothes burned, and some do not. If one learns nothing else from the study of the occult, one at least learns not to expect consistency.

Self-scarification

These reservations also apply in the case of what might be called ritual self-scarification. This again is a widespread and long-standing phenomenon. However, oriental self-scarification differs again significantly from that practised by Africans, Pacific Islanders and Christian ascetics, in that its purpose is not to damage the body of the celebrant, but to demonstrate his occult capacity to resist damage. Here once more there is no lack of evidence and corroboration. The most systematic form of this art is undoubtedly that performed by Chinese worshippers of the various spirit-medium cults of Singapore. Practically everything has been documented except the exact nature of what it is that they worship. In the most basic terms, the object of their ritual is to placate a divine being called a *shen*, a term which offers as many problems to the translator as *ch'i*, in that it seems to mean either 'soul', 'a spirit' (supernatural being), or 'force', possibly in the sense of intrinsic energy.

Shens naturally behave according to laws which are not those of this world, and are in consequence unpredictable: they can inhabit any spot of land, and can inhabit the body of any person. What is agreed upon is that the effect of possession by a *shen* is that the *yang* element of one's spiritual body is displaced by the *shen*, and that this possession is quite independent of the will of the person concerned. This person then becomes as it were a medium for the *shen*. His role could be said to be an honoured one, since he is the one to whom believers will look to placate the particular *shen* which possesses him. It has on the other hand considerable disadvantages as the medium or *dang-ki* ('divining youth') is required to live a pure life, for fear of offending the *shen*; is not allowed to perform for gain, although he may of course receive gifts which have to be made freely by the worshippers, and may not be sought; and he usually dies young.

Virtually the whole of the rituals performed by the *dang-ki* consist in demonstrations of the power of the *shen* to protect him from physical injury. His equipment accordingly reads like a list of the contents of a mediaeval torture chamber. It begins with a black flag on which the Eight Trigrams of pa-kua are emblazoned in gold. Then there is the prick-ball, a metal ball studded with 108 metal spikes, which the *dang-ki* will swing at either his back or stomach; a set of metal skewers six inches long, with ornamented wooden heads ('generals' heads') which he will thrust through his own cheeks and neck; a set of silver needles with elaborate metalwork heads, which he will use to penetrate the arms of his assistants; and most impressively a 'knife-chair', with blades or sharp spikes on the back, seat, and arm- and foot-rests, on which the *dang-ki* will be carried in procession. Further articles of worship could include a sword for cutting the *dang-ki*'s tongue; a ladder for him to climb, with sharp blades for steps; and a table with fixed and rotating spikes and knife-blades for him to roll around on.

It is of course what the *dang-ki* does with these instruments that counts. Western investigators have again found themselves confronted with a combination of what could certainly be called deception and what can only be called inexplicable in material terms. The unsatisfactory aspects can be mentioned at once. It has consistently been noted that the *dang-ki* is extremely sparing in his use of the prick-ball, trying to ensure that the spikes barely touch the flesh of back or stomach. It has also been noted that where the *dang-ki* has been insufficiently cautious, the spikes have drawn blood and left scars. There seems to be no immunity there. Nor does the *dang-ki* exactly seem to be immune from the effect of cutting his tongue to draw blood, with which to smear the charm papers which will be used to convey honour and supplications to his *shen*. It is of course necessary that his tongue should actually bleed, and on all the evidence it bleeds as profusely as one might expect, and heals with uncomfortable ridges of scar-tissue. It is also perhaps unfortunate that when the *dang-ki* employs the skewers on himself, his head is usually hidden with pa-kua flags, so that the laity cannot actually see what is happening. They can certainly see the after-effects, however. The skewers are inserted either through the mouth into the cheek; or through both cheeks; or through the throat directly above the adam's apple, the skin being pressed into a fold before insertion. In the case of the *dang-ki*'s assistants, the skewers are normally stuck through the fleshy part of the upper arm. Both *dang-ki* and assistants remain skewered during the service, which may take a matter of hours. The skewers are then withdrawn by pressing hard on the skin about the point of entry, and pulling swiftly. The withdrawn skewer usually leaves some traces of bleeding, though nothing like as much as one might normally expect, and this is stopped almost at once by pressing with the thumb.

On the other hand, the claim that the skewering does not leave a scar is demonstrably untrue, as most *dang-ki* soon acquire a disagreeably pock-marked appearance from their skewering. However, they appear to feel no pain; they certainly show minimal bleeding; and the way in which they perform their religious duties of meditation shows that they are perfectly in command of their senses, and not in any condition of shock or trance. Western observers have also confirmed that the body of the *dang-ki* does in fact become abnormally cold, as claimed by tradition, at the moment that he is possessed by his *shen*. There is also no doubt that *dang-kis* go through the rituals of being carried in the knife-chairs and extended on the knife-tables without being cut by the blades. The suggested explanation that they somehow manage to distribute their weight so that they are not perforated by sharp edges and points really lacks conviction. It must also be remembered that these feats are not performed on stages, with distracting lights, music and all the resources for trickery available to the western magician: they are performed outside, in broad daylight, with observers and photographers swarming around, in conditions which provide the maximum opportunity to detect any attempt at fraud.

The feats of the *dang-ki* are of course no more remarkable than those of the masters of the martial arts which we have already considered, and which can similarly be explained away neither as frauds nor hypnotism. Nor are they more remarkable than the achievements of Indian yogis who lie on beds of nails and sword-edges in public; and who were seen by Paul Brunton to thrust skewers through their open mouths so that they came out of their cheeks, and to pull out their own eyeballs so that they hung loosely against their cheekbones. Fr Gonzalez-Quevado has also demonstrated his ability to thrust a skewer through his forearm or neck, above the adam's apple, and to insert the blade of a knife under his eyelid, without injury or bleeding.

Acupuncture

One might indeed find it difficult to suggest exactly what purpose is served by these feats of self-scarification, except to show that they can be done. However, there are no such reservations about the related practice of acupuncture. The probability is indeed that this oldest of medical sciences may well make most other methods obsolete. Ninety per cent of all operations performed in Canton at present are done by acupuncture, and the

method has already been used in England. There is indeed
nothing obscure about the techniques of acupuncture. The
Chinese have always been perfectly willing to allow foreigners
to observe its use, in total contrast to their attitude towards the
martial arts. Nothing could be simpler. Gold and silver needles
are inserted in particular spots on the patient's body. That is all.
What does need a little explaining is exactly what happens
after they have been inserted.

Acupuncture appears to have been used originally in the
treatment of what might rather inexactly be called nervous
complaints, such as rheumatoid arthritis, epilepsy and certain
kinds of deafness. Its chief employment at present is probably as
an anaesthetic. Its effect in this field can only be called mir-
aculous.

Australian parliamentarians visiting Peking in July 1971
were taken to see a number of operations by acupuncture carried out by Dr Chang Tzu-sun, under the direction of Dr Chou
Kuan-han. They saw, among other things, a man singing and
quoting inspirational passages from Chairman Mao while the
doctors removed his appendix; another patient talking ani-
matedly while his gall bladder was taken out; an older woman
laughing and explaining how she was going to make new pro-
duction records at her factory while having an ovarian cyst removed; and an ancient grandfather get off the operating table
by himself and walk to the trolley which was to take him back
to his bed, after a cataract operation. There was clearly no
question of hypnosis, as the patients were fully conscious all the
time. Nor could this immunity from either pain or physical
shock be attributed to auto-suggestion, as the patients clearly
did not prepare themselves psychologically in any way for the
experience. It was all matter-of-fact, and quite inexplicable,
according to any of the principles of conventional western
medical science. It was beyond debate that the patients did
indeed feel no pain during these operations: the only abnormal
physical sensation any of them mentioned was a vague feeling
of 'heaviness' after the needles had been inserted.

Australian doctors found the whole business quite unaccountable. It was not just that the acupuncture treatment obviously operated as a totally effective local anaesthetic in some quite uncomprehended manner. Even more extraordinary was the fact that it appeared to eliminate not only the physical side-effects of a normal anaesthetic, but also at least most of the physical shock of the actual operation itself. Further evidence was however provided by an Australian businessman, Mr Alex Encel, who visited Canton after the parliamentarians had returned home. There he witnessed an operation on a twenty-eight-year-old woman for removal of a cyst in her thyroid gland. One needle was inserted into her leg, just above the knee, and a second into her wrist. A nurse agitated the two needles for about five minutes; a surgeon opened the woman's throat; a cyst the size of an egg was snipped off; the wound in the throat was sewn up; and the patient, whose only physical reaction had been to blink once at the moment that the cyst was snipped off, sat up, smiled, and resumed talking.

Mr Encel saw two further operations, one for a Caesarean birth, and one for the removal of a kidney stone. In both cases, the patients remained fully conscious, were quite unaffected by the immensely painful operations, and talked cheerfully with the nurses the whole time.

It is not usually necessary to multiply examples of the impossible: one verified instance is sufficient to prove any point worth making. But there is the particular interest in each individual example of acupuncture surgery, that it serves to emphasize the apparently total effectiveness of the technique. The most astounding examples are undoubtedly those quoted by the English Dr Percy Brown, who described in the most prestigious of medical journals, *The Lancet*, how he saw Chinese doctors remove a tumour from a man's brain, while he remained fully conscious. On this occasion, needles connected to a nine-volt battery were inserted into the patient's thumb, jaw, right leg, left forearm and forehead. A far less complex system was used on another patient to whom Dr Brown fed segments of an orange, while a tuberculous growth was removed from his right lung. Here the only anaesthetic was a needle inserted in the right biceps. The patient said he enjoyed the orange.

It can conservatively be asserted that acupuncture works. *The Lancet* itself considers that the technique definitely merits investigation. The difficulty as always is to find out what exactly is working. The Chinese doctors themselves were distinctly vague. However, traditional Chinese teaching is as usual quite explicit. Acupuncture is based on the concept of the *ch'i*. Points on the surface of the skin less than a millimetre wide act as pathways through which intrinsic energy flows to the internal organs of the human bodies. Needles inserted in the body at these points can correct any irregularities or imbalances in the flow of intrinsic energy to the organs.

This technique could apparently be used for diagnostic purposes in classical times. A doctor skilled in acupuncture therapy would be able to detect any such irregularities in the movement of intrinsic energy in a patient's body, and could therefore predict exactly in which of his organs the patient would be afflicted, unless the flow of intrinsic energy were changed. There was thus a scientific basis so to speak for the classical practice under which the patient paid the doctor for keeping him from falling sick, and the doctor paid the patient if his prophylaxis failed.

The basis would be scientific if there were any reason to believe that these 'acupuncture points' actually exist. It is certain that they have never been located by dissection. There is also unfortunately considerable disagreement among both the Indians and the Chinese as to exactly how many of these points there are, and exactly where they are located. Raja-yoga, for example, settles for seven nerve-centres, in which intrinsic energy is stored in the body; shorinji kempo teaches that intrinsic energy travels along fourteen routes through the body, along which there are 708 'holes' or 'switches'; acupuncture charts actually available now list some seventeen or eighteen main and branch channels, with about 221 points for therapy.

This uncertainty about the number and perhaps even the location of the acupuncture points might well give rise to some misgivings. These are made the more serious by the fact that the Chinese themselves do not always seem to put their needle in what would appear to be the most logical places, to judge from available accounts of operations. It is for example not clear why a needle inserted in the wrist or the leg should have any effect on feeling in the throat. Nor is it clear why a needle in the biceps should influence the flow of *ch'i* on that side of the chest, since according to the acupuncture charts, the *ch'i* should flow through the chest to the arm, rather than the other way about. As so often happens in the study of mind over matter, the techniques employed seem so completely arbitrary, various and sometimes illogical, that one can only ask oneself if the techniques really matter at all. It may not make any difference where the Chinese put their needles.

On the other hand, it may. Soviet science has come to the rescue here, to some extent at least. It has been shown finally in Russian laboratories that the body does in fact produce energy of some kind or other, in the form of vibrations which can be detected by electronic apparatus. Moreover, photographs can be taken of substances, including the human body, by the use of high-frequency electrical fields, which cause the substances exposed to them to radiate 'bio-luminescence' on to photo-sensitized paper. Pictures taken under these conditions reveal that the vibrations produced by the human body appear as patterns of multi-coloured flares. These flares in fact show up as points of brilliant light on spots corresponding to some at least of the points marked on the body for acupuncture therapy in traditional Chinese medicine. It may indeed make quite a lot of difference just where the Chinese put their needles. Once again, the most advanced western science appears to be merely demonstrating and finding its own explanations for the fundamental reality of traditional oriental wisdom.

Conclusion: *how is it done?*

In 1960 Professor H. J. Eysenck, one of the most influential of British psychologists, said in words that have to provide the favourite quotation of parapsychologists and students of the occult:

Unless there is a gigantic conspiracy involving some thirty university departments all over the world, and several hundred highly respected scientists in various fields, the only conclusion the unbiased observer can come to must be that there does exist a small number of people who obtain knowledge existing either in other people's minds, or in the outer world, by means as yet unknown to science.

One can only say that this was a conservative statement even in 1960. The situation is quite different now. The 'thirty universities' have mushroomed. The number of highly respected scientists involved has expanded to thousands. The number of scientific publications on various branches of parapsychology in the Soviet Union alone has increased from two to over seventy in the past fourteen years. But these numbers themselves represent only the tip of the iceberg. As we have seen, it is in the fields of the martial arts, yoga and oriental medicine that the most convincing and reliable demonstrations of mind over matter have been achieved, and the number of people actively involved in the esoteric areas of these arts can reasonably be assumed to approach at least the million mark.

One conclusion at least can be made at once: there is no way in the world in which these varied manifestations can be explained away as hallucinations implanted by skilled mass hypnotists. There are too many cameras around, too many electronic recording devices and too many piles of broken bricks and tiles for the hypnosis hypothesis to be acceptable any more. That leaves two possibilities. The first is that huge numbers of immensely sophisticated and respected scientists in every country in the world, plus literally all the most revered yogis of India and Tibet, the people most esteemed in the world for their spiritual and moral qualities, along with all the most revered masters of the martial arts of the orient, are and always have been lying unremittingly to one another and to everybody else on this particular topic. This would be on all counts the most impressive accusation of dishonesty ever made. It would also be immensely the most improbable. It is nonetheless the only basis on which the argument of the sceptics can be maintained.

One might well feel that an argument which has to be maintained on these grounds takes too much maintaining altogether. It is however not quite so easy to see what one is left with. Simply, our investigations seem to indicate that a very considerable number of people in all parts of the world, but particularly in Asia, possess the ability to influence external objects through the exercise of their mental powers, and that this capacity is in most cases acquired or at least developed through the practice of physical exercises which differ wildly from school to school, but which all have in common an emphasis on muscular relaxation and abdominal breathing. That would be something to start with. However, one also has to admit that these powers seem to be possessed by other people outside of Asia who do not appear even to have heard of the Asian arts of physical culture. They may of course simply be natural mental athletes, or they may just serve to prove that there are different routes to the same goal.

Obviously, one cannot be dogmatic about how these powers are acquired, unless one really knows what they are. Here western science does in fact seem largely to have confirmed eastern tradition. Russian high-frequency field experiments have established that the human body does in fact produce energy, and that this radiates from the surface of the body at the acupuncture points, and therefore probably travels through the body along the channels through which the *ch'i* is supposed to flow. It is no more surprising that these channels cannot be discovered by physiological examination, than it is that the channels of force in a magnet cannot be discovered by examining it under a microscope.

So the body produces energy. It also produces it in different amounts at different times. The English Dr Grey Walker has demonstrated by means of an encephalograph that the brain does indeed produce electrical 'waves', and that the magnetic effect of these waves is noticeably greater in parapsychological conditions, when precognition, telepathy or telekinesis are being exerted, than in normal conditions. The 'waves' of the brain in fact vary in frequency and magnitude according to the kind of thought experienced by the subject.

Fr Gonzalez-Quevado has produced a theory which reconciles these factors fairly satisfactorily, as well as having the additional advantage of being generally consistent with his own theological presuppositions. He makes in the first place a distinction between genuine theological miracles, which can be performed by God alone, and feats performed by the use of occult powers which are strictly human, being natural to man, though it would seem natural to his spiritual rather than to his physical self. The distinction may not seem wholly satisfactory to everybody, but in any case it does not affect the development of Fr Gonzalez-Quevado's argument. He says that a force exists in the physical world which is not limited entirely by the conditions of that world. He calls it 'telergia' (*tele*: 'long', *ergon*: 'work') after the word invented by Frederic Myers. He also considers this power to be not supernatural but *extra-ordinario-normais*, which may be translated simply as 'exceptional', in the sense that a person gifted in any other field of human endeavour can be said to be exceptional, without being regarded as inhuman or even as a freak. Fr Gonzalez-Quevado accordingly considers telergia or intrinsic energy to be material and physical.

There can be no question that the whole point of this study is to suggest that there is such a force and that it can operate in a material way. Nor is there any doubt that an increasing number of scientists claim that they are able to detect its presence and even to photograph it with sophisticated electronic equipment. Again, a fundamental tenet of Chinese and Indian teaching is that this force is limited in its efficacy by the nature of the physical body of the person employing it. On the other hand, the effect of these physical limitations is none too clear, to put it mildly. Fr Gonzalez-Quevado affirms that telergia is simply a kind of electricity which is not limited by the same physical factors as electricity in the normal sense: it is in fact 'bio-electricity'. He is thus in fact adopting much the same concept as Mesmer's notion of 'animal magnetism', or a 'universal fluid', which could be directed from one body to another and could act upon it in a manner similar to that of ordinary magnetism.

Mesmer did indeed stumble on to something corresponding to the oriental notion of the human body as a tai-chi, when he conceived of it as a magnet, with two poles, represented by its two sides. Disease was caused by some imbalance in the proper distribution of the magnetic fluid, just as the Chinese masters of acupuncture believe that disease is the consequence of imbalances in the movement of intrinsic energy. Mesmer, however, seems also to have believed that the magnetic fluid could operate at a distance, be reflected by mirrors, be contained in bottles for export and be somehow transferred to impersonal or inanimate objects, such as trees.

One can easily believe that Mesmer did not fully know what he was talking about, although his ideas might well seem rather less comical now than they would have seemed a few years ago. It may not be possible to bottle intrinsic energy, but it does stream from the hands of the subject, as Mesmer imagined; it does operate at a distance, in telekinesis, levitation and perhaps kiai-jutsu; and it has at least this much resemblance to a fluid, that it circulates through the body and can possibly be exteriorized as a kind of jelly-like mist in manifestations of ectoplasm.

In any event, Fr Gonzalez-Quevado suggests that what he

prefers to call 'bio-electricity' can be transformed into para-psychological effects, which are in fact caused by the escape of 'bio-electricity' from the body. He calls this a 'psychorrhage' to indicate that it is as much a natural phenomenon as the escape of blood, or 'haemorrhage'. Being natural, it can take place only over a limited range, and can be circumscribed in its effects by purely natural factors.

It certainly seems as if some of the earlier tests in clairvo-yance or telekinesis did suggest that distance might have had some effect upon the occult powers of the subjects. However, so many other features of these tests were inconclusive, that one could not dare to deduce much from them. Telepathy at least seems to be subject to no physical limitations at all: the Soviets claim to have sent telepathic coded messages from Moscow to Tomsk, 3,000 miles away, and are certainly attempting to de-velop telepathy as a means of communication with cosmonauts in space. The US Navy was supposed to have used similar experiments during the under-sea and under-the-pole voyage of the *Nautilus*, but this has been officially denied.

There does at least seem every possibility that the actual power of intrinsic energy to influence material objects in the physical universe is subject to some limitations. Chinese and Indian boxers can apparently splinter bricks without effort; but they have not yet tried to punch their way through steel plates. Yogis can, it seems, levitate themselves and other human beings; they are not reported as having levitated eleph-ants. The Tibetans of course claim to be able to work unlimited miracles, but one has yet to see the Tibetans work anything under reasonably strict control conditions. The fact is that faith and telergia really do not seem to be able to move mountains, although we may believe that they can raise a table with two Argentine professors sitting on it.

Fr Gonzalez-Quevado suggests twelve feet as about the limit for the operation of telergia over distance. All reported ac-counts of levitation do in fact seem to have taken place within less than this distance. An interesting experiment which may help to support this theory was carried out in the Soviet Union, when electronic detectors registered force fields radiating from Mrs Mikhailova up to a distance of twelve feet. Detectors registered a similar escape of energy from the bodies of clinically dead persons at the same distance.

These experiments naturally raise further complications. It seems that energy flows from the body at death in the same way in which it leaves the body during the exercise of occult powers. Death becomes a phenomenon of parapsychology. Moreover, other experiments of this nature seem to provide scientific support for some of what seem to be the most fanciful notions of both Indian yoga and western spiritualism: that the body is surrounded by an aura and in fact possesses duplicates of itself which function in different universes.

Mrs Eileen Garrett, President of the Parapsychology Foundation of New York, has claimed to be able to 'see' the auras of people she meets without the aid of instruments. It is however difficult to be sure that people are in fact seeing anything if it is not apparent at the same time to others. Dr Walter Kilner at St Thomas's Hospital, London, had similarly claimed, in 1900, that he had been able to see radiation patterns emanating from human bodies when viewed through glass screens stained with dicyanin dye.

The Russians, however, have actually taken photographs. Valentina and Semyon Kirlian carried out experiments in photography with high-frequency fields in Krasnodar, which recorded images which suggest not only that the human body has an aura, but that this aura of radiation in fact forms an exact counterpart of every aspect of the physical body. We thus apparently have at least two bodies to get along with: the physical one with which we are familiar and an energy force-field which is a mirror image of our physical body, and which would therefore correspond to the 'astral body' beloved of mystics. The Kirlians' investigations have been enthusiastically supported by members of the USSR Academy of Sciences, the Moscow Medical Institute and the Kirov State University of Kazahkistan, which is actually investigating the possibilities of astral projection, or out-of-the-body travel, per medium of this energy 'self'. The word impossible has really ceased to have much significance in Russia at least.

These discoveries of investigations both support and to some degree question the analysis of Fr Gonzalez-Quevado. In the first place, they unquestionably provide further basis for his argument that occult powers are in fact natural to man, who presumably lost knowledge of them with the Fall. However, they make it harder than ever to draw any kind of line between occult powers natural to man, and supernatural powers possessed only by God. Fr Gonzalez-Quevado argues that a truly supernatural force, such as that exercised by God in the performance of His miracles, would not be subject to any limitations of distance or effect, such as human occult powers seem to be. However, the fact is that we really do not know what the limits of the use of intrinsic energy in the physical universe actually are. We accordingly do not know what particular feat, regarded by Fr Gonzalez-Quevado as a miracle performance by God, might not have been effected by the human use of occult powers. What we do know is that the analogies between intrinsic energy or telergia and material of imperfectly comprehended forces like electricity or magnetism, merely serve to illustrate the colossal differences between the two kinds of energy. If telergia works at all, it works on substances which are not conductors of energy, and it is not interrupted by nonconductors. It also has to be remembered that the amount of electrical power generated by the human brain is totally inadequate to produce the effects we have been considering: the electrical discharges produced by subjects under parapsychological conditions have for example to be magnified four million times before they can even be recorded.

There is also the difficulty that telergia can apparently be used for any purpose which the subject desires, while there are still things that electricity cannot do: it cannot for example prevent one from being bruised when one is hammered with a hardwood stave, or prevent one from feeling pain during an internal operation. One can only assume that telergia really cannot be purely physical in its nature or origin, although the effect of its operation in the physical universe is apparently subject to some limitation by physical factors. It is really far more likely that electricity or magnetism are manifestations of intrinsic energy, rather than that intrinsic energy is a form of electricity and magnetism. We are once again forced right back to the interpretations of the yogis and the masters of the martial arts.

We are forced back to them in another way as well. One of the major difficulties in the way of discovering some central core of doctrine among the various oriental schools was of course the bewildering variety of ways in which they claimed that intrinsic energy could be acquired. It was even more bewildering when one considered that intrinsic energy seems to have been acquired at times by westerners who might never even have heard of the oriental arts. However, it seems now as if one is justified in suggesting that the essential element is in fact the emphasis on the avoidance of any involuntary motion, tension or distracting thought. The *ch'i* simply cannot move if body and mind are not under full control of the will. Tests with encephalographs on subjects claiming to possess occult powers have in fact indicated that their powers function most effectively only when in a condition of maximum mental and physical repose and receptivity. This condition is exactly what the contortions of hatha-yoga, the spiritual exercises of raja-yoga, the incredibly slow and deliberate movements of tai-chi ch'uan, the agonizing rigidities of the horse-back stance, the sustained muscular contractions of pa-kua are all designed to produce, by developing total mental and physical discipline. There are evidently other, less painful and perhaps quite involuntary ways of achieving the same result, but the goal is unchanged. Intrinsic energy rises in a state of calmness, free from all tensions or restraints on freedom of movement or response. It can take years of intense effort to learn to achieve a true state of relaxation. On the other hand, it may also be possible that one can brush away any inhibiting tensions or distractions by a quite untutored exercise of the will, so that we would be able to call on the powers of intrinsic energy literally without knowing that we were doing so.

This could certainly have rather alarming implications. Here again the Asians have obviously thought of it all before. Occult powers of mind over matter could present humanity with immensely serious problems, at a time when it does seem particularly capable of solving the problems it is confronted with already. Mind over matter means that we live in a world in which people can do things with their bodies which their bodies are not physically capable of doing: they can smash bricks with their uncalloused hands, transmit energy to produce delayed effects, resist the force of other men far stronger than themselves, raise themselves and others off the ground, walk on fire without being burned, cut themselves without bleeding, submit their bodies to fearful blows without suffering pain or damage, make inanimate objects move at command, cure the afflicted with a shout, control their heartbeats and their respiration, and ignore the cold of the Himalayas. They appear to be able to do many other extraordinary things as well, but we can take these that are sufficiently proved for any practical purpose.

Nor do we know how many people can acquire these powers. The Rhines have suggested that one person in five might possess powers of extra-sensory perception, but this can be only a guess. Unless the whole notion of telergia or intrinsic energy is wrong, these qualities are natural to man and probably to living beings in general, so that anything that lives has at least the potentiality to develop them to some degree. There may be all manner of reasons, mental, temperamental or physical why in fact only a certain proportion may be able to develop them to a significant degree, in the sense that almost anybody with two legs can run, but not everybody has the physique or powers of concentration or even desire to be able to learn how to run a mile in four minutes.

What seems to emerge from all this is that many of us at least have access to powers which are virtually independent of the laws of the physical universe; that we cannot be entirely sure how these powers are called into operation; and we certainly cannot be sure what effect they might be having on our lives, without our being aware of it. It would be as well to find out. If parapsychology is a reality, then no other study can begin to compare with it in importance.

What also emerges is that the foundations of both conventional science and conventional religion are seriously called in question by the human use of intrinsic energy. One need not worry too much about conventional science, as its foundations have in fact been abandoned by many scientists long since. One is now confronted with a universe in which it makes only very limited sense to talk of physical laws. We have to deal with particles which have in fact no properties, and have even had to conceive of the possibility of the existence of anti-matter, forming a universe as real as the one our instruments and senses recognize, but being physically undetectable. It is therefore at least possible that different universes co-exist with one another, and to some extent overlap, so that one can in fact be functioning in more than one at a time. One might mention that the whole idea of precognition, which can at least hardly be doubted except by the most unreconstructed sceptic, depends absolutely upon the notion of diverse universes. One cannot possibly be aware of a happening unless it has actually happened: one cannot 'see' the future unless the future has taken place somewhere. Precognition thus demands a world in which everything that will happen is happening all the time somewhere, and everything that has already happened is still happening all the time somewhere else.

Religion presents more problems, simply because of the dogmatic nature of Christianity. It must be admitted that the study of mind over matter does little to support the notion of a personal God. It suggests rather that any paranormal happenings piously attributed to divine intervention could well have taken place as a result of the human use of intrinsic energy. It also makes embarrassingly clear that eastern religions have been far more successful in coping with the problems of the occult than western Christianity, and can therefore be regarded as no less divine in origin, to say the least. Finally, it seems that visions of divine beings are literally conjured up by the visionary, who fabricates out of intrinsic energy precisely the form of divinity which he wishes to see.

This has perhaps the most serious implication of all. If we can conjure up gods, we can also conjure up devils. It is indeed probable that any concept or desire which we have concentrated on long or intensely enough may well be conjured into being in some universe of mental energy into which we could be projected ourselves when intrinsic energy escapes finally from the physical body at death. The prospect of having to live in a universe populated by our own desires, or by the desires of others whose lives have influenced ours, at least suggest that one might be advised to be careful what one thinks about.

Here too the Asians appear to have been far more systematic and clear-sighted than conventional western religion. The conventional Christian veto on dealings with the occult has at least this much to be said for it: in dealing with the occult, we are dealing with powers which we are of necessity inadequately equipped to handle. It would not be surprising if they accordingly get out of control in the physical universe, especially in view of our limited success in coping with our physical resources. On the other hand, it is equally unrealistic to try to leave them strictly alone: if all the cases we have looked at prove anything, it is that we are indeed amphibians, as was suggested in the introduction, inhabiting two worlds simultaneously, a physical world which we recognize with our senses, and a world of intrinsic energy which is not physical in its origin or nature. It behoves us to tread warily, and at the same time to try to learn the rules. This is of course what the Asians have always done. If there is one thing common to both yoga and the martial arts, it is their insistence on the most complete mastery of thought and action; their concentration on the enduring rather than the transient; their absolute rejection of anything suggesting impatience, presumption or aggressiveness; and their commitment to dedication, discipline and universal harmony. The West is not likely to be able to improve on Asian teaching here. In the field of mind over matter at least, the role of western science and technology has been to confirm and find new terms for the traditional wisdom of the East.

Notes

Introduction
1 Oscar Gonzalez-Quevado, *As Forcas Fisicas da Mente* (Edi-ções Loyola, São Paulo, 1968).

Chapter 1

1 *Black Belt Magazine* (August 1966).
2 See John F. Gilbey, *Secret Fighting Arts of the World* (Prentice Hall, New York, 1963). This remarkable book has been denounced ever since its appearance either as a work of fantasy, or for its lack of informative detail. It has, however, been pointed out by Asian students that Dr Gilbey would not have been allowed to see as much as he did, unless he had promised beforehand not to tell more than he has. Moreover, many of the arts described by Gilbey have been shown subsequently to be unquestionably factual. For example, E. J. Harrison, who is indeed no fantasist, corroborates Gilbey's accounts of *kiai-jutsu*; Robert W. Smith has produced material which complements Gilbey's revelations about *hsing-i*; *Black Belt Magazine* is investigating new data about the 'delayed death touch'; and what Gilbey calls 'the dinky little poke' is nothing more or less than the totally factual and effective Wing Chun punch. All in all, *Secret Fighting Arts of the World* can only be regarded as still one of the basic texts in the field of the occult martial arts.
3 See E. J. Harrison, *The Fighting Spirit of Japan* (Foulsham, New York, 1960), an immensely comprehensive and authoritative work by one of the greatest western students of the oriental arts.
4 Robert W. Smith, *Asian Fighting Arts* (Ohara Publications, Los Angeles, 1969). The most comprehensive, informative and literate work on the Asian martial arts.

5 For appropriate comments, see *Black Belt Magazine* (August 1969).
6 As for example recommended by sifu Bruce Lee, *Black Belt Magazine* (October 1967).

Chapter 2

1 B. Fawcett, *Operation Fawcett* (Hutchinson, London, 1958).
2 E. J. Harrison, *The Fighting Spirit of Japan* (Foulsham, New York, 1960).
3 W. Y. Evans-Wentz, *Tibet's Great Yogi Milrepa* (Clarendon, Oxford, 1966).
4 A. Caycedo, *India of Yogis* (National Publishing House, Delhi, 1966).
5 See Jay Gluck, *Zen Combat* (Ballantine, New York, 1962). The earliest, and still one of the most comprehensive and most perceptive of all studies in English of the oriental martial arts.
6 M. Oyama, *This is Karate* (Martial Arts Supply Company, Los Angeles, 1964). Oyama's books are the most magnificently produced, informed, detailed and authoritative statements of the development of classical karate.

Chapter 3

1 *Black Belt Magazine* (March 1972).
2 G. H. Estabrooks, *Hypnotism* (Dutton, New York, 1957).

Chapter 4

1 Norman Mailer, *A Fire on The Moon* (Weidenfeld and Nicolson, London, 1970 and Pan, London, 1971).
2 Robert W. Smith, *Pa-kua* (Ward Lock, London, 1967). This book should have made history as the first substantial study in English or a major branch of Chinese boxing, utterly unlike any other form of self-defence. One of its most interesting features to the student of the martial arts is the clarity with which it indicates the difference between what the Chinese practise for physical and spiritual development, and the techniques they actually use when fighting. There is still no other comprehensive and realistic study of this kind around.

Chapter 5

1 Sri Aurobindo, *The Mind of Light* (Dutton, New York, 1971).
2 Dr V. M. Bhat, *Yogic Powers and God Realisation* (Bharatiya Vidya Bhavan, Bombay, 1960).
3 K. Amis, *The Green Man* (Cape, London, 1969).
4 E. Y. Evans-Wentz, *Tibetan Yoga* (Oxford University Press, 1959).
5 P. H. Pott, *Yoga and Yantra* (Martinus Nijhoff, The Hague, 1966).
6 Sir Paul Duke, *The Yoga of Health, Youth and Joy* (Cassell, London, 1960).
7 A. Puharich, *Beyond Telepathy* (Longmans, London, 1962).
8 A. L. Basham, *The Wonder that was India* (Sidgwick & Jackson, London, 1962).
9 *Journal of the Society for Psychical Research* (March 1964).
10 J. B. Rhine and J. G. Pratt, *Parapsychology* (Charles C. Thomas, Springfield, 1957).
11 A. David-Neil, *Magic and Mystery in Tibet* (Souvenir Press, London, 1961).
12 P. Brunton, *The Hidden Teaching Beyond Yoga* (Rider, London, 1962).

Chapter 6

1 Ernest Wood, *Yoga* (Cassell, London, 1962).
2 Dr V. M. Bhat, *Yogic Powers and God Realisation* (Bharatiya Vidya Bhavan, Bombay, 1960).

Bibliography

Introduction

A consideration of individual criticisms of the study of the occult is beyond the scope of this book and a list of books for or against would be endless. The following, however, might be listed among the more significant of recent publications:

Milbourne Christopher, *Ghosts, Poltergeists and ESP* (Cassell, London, 1971)

O. Gonzalez-Quevado, *A Face Oculta da Mente* (Edicões Loyola, São Paulo, 1967)

R. Heywood, *The Sixth Sense* (Pan, London, 1967)

D. Hunt, *Exploring the Occult* (Pan, London, 1971)

A. Koestler, *The Roots of Coincidence* (Hutchinson, London, 1972 and Picador, London, 1974)

D. H. Rawcliffe, *Illusions and Delusions of the Supernatural and the Occult* (Dover Publications, New York, 1959)

J. B. Rhine, *Progress in Parapsychology* (Parapsychology Press, Durham, 1971)

Louisa Rhine, *Mind Over Matter* (Macmillan, New York, 1970)

C. Wilson, *The Occult* (Hodder and Stoughton, London, 1971)

Chapter 1

Books dealing with judo as a sport do not really come within the scope of this study. Nor do books which attempt to adapt elaborately impractical judo techniques to actual situations of self-defence. The most philosophically rewarding or practically useful studies would include:

Pat Butler, *Self-Defence Complete* (Emerson, New York, 1962), a thoroughly reliable guide to most practical varieties of dirty fighting, particularly valuable for its sane advice on how to cope with attack by an experienced boxer, and for its passage on self-defence with an umbrella, adapted from army bayonet-fighting drills. Perfectionists might suggest only that it is perhaps safer to kick straight forward for the kneecap or the groin, rather than to use the slower side-kick suggested, and that one really needs a fairly robust umbrella for this kind of work. However, this deserves the highest praise among works on self-defence, as an informative study which is more likely to get one out of trouble, than into it.

Ching-nan Lee and Ruben Figueroa, *Techniques of Self-Defence* (Barnes, New York, 1963). The best matter-of-fact work on jiu-jitsu, outstanding for its success in imposing a system on the most unsystematic albeit one of the most reliable of the martial arts. Its message, for use on all occasions, might be summarized: hit him in the face and move in circles. It could almost be said that if this doesn't work, nothing else will. There are really no better hand techniques than those depicted here. It is admittedly quite unphilosophical, and almost never uses the feet or knees aggressively.

Chapter 2

The literature on karate, both in monograph form and in periodicals, is again almost excessive in quantity. One can only recommend the excellent periodicals *Black Belt Magazine, Karate Illustrated* and *Karate and Oriental Arts* for their informed style, and particularly for their balance between practical combat techniques and the esoteric side of the martial arts. Other authors who can always be consulted with profit are Draeger, Nakayama, Parker, and of course E. J. Harrison. The authoritative book on shorinji kempo is the study of that name by sensei Doshin So, a book which does for this probably superior art all that Oyama's books do for karate. Shorinji kempo undoubtedly represents the finest distillation of the Chinese and Japanese arts, with a useful infusion of western boxing. One's only reservation might be that some of the Chinese arts are even more effective undistilled. It is, for example, difficult to see why the shorinji kempo masters adhere to the stop-go, block-and-then-punch Japanese techniques, instead of the simultaneously two-handed approach of aikido and Chinese boxing. However, the Indians, who appear to have been involved in the martial arts longer than anybody else, also seem to block and punch alternately.

Chapter 3

Almost everything written on aikido represents a serious contribution to both the martial arts and the study of occultism. Some
of the more substantial works include:

Gozo Shioda, *Dynamic Aikido* (Ward Lock & Co., London,
1968), perhaps the least esoteric and most compactly practical
book on aikido;

Koichi Tohei, *Aikido* (Charles E. Tuttle, Rutland, 1960);

Kisshomaru Uyeshiba, *Aikido* (Hoyansha, Tokyo, 1972).

All these books expound the philosophy and techniques of the
safest and generally most effective of systems of self-defence. It
must however be admitted that none of them specifically explain
how one actually puts an opponent out of action after pinning
him, and the problem of dealing with a fast western-type boxer
is never really dealt with. The first problem is not really serious:
one simply breaks his arm in three places. The second is perhaps
the only important deficiency of this wonderful art. The reader
must of course realize that the techniques recommended by Tohei
against an opponent armed with a knife will work *only* if one has
developed occult powers of precognition. If one has any doubt
about how well one's *ki* is operating in such a situation, the only
advice is really to throw something at your assailant to blind him,
charge him with a chair or get a weapon with a longer reach
than his blade.

Chapter 4

Robert W. Smith, *Secrets of Shao-lin Temple Boxing* (Tuttle,
Tokyo, 1964). Dr Smith says in this book that there are no good
books on Shao-lin, only varying degrees of bad. This was before
his own contributions to the study of the Chinese martial arts,
which remain the most informative, well-written and clearly
illustrated works in a field which is still by no means over-
crowded.

Yerning K. Chen, *Tai-Chi Ch'uan* (Martial Arts Supplies, Los
Angeles), the most philosophical and detailed study in English
of tai-chi ch'uan, with extremely full and completely incredible
descriptions of how the movements are adapted to actual combat
situations. One can only say that tai-chi ch'uan fighters seem to
short-circuit these motions very much indeed.

Cheng-man Ching, *Tai-Chi Ch'uan* (Shih Cheung, Taipei). A much-simplified and therefore probably much more practical description of the basic moves of tai-chi, with a most interesting historical background. There is, however, virtually no indication as to how these movements might be adapted to a self-defence situation, although some at least have in fact an extremely direct application. For example, the exercise innocently called 'raising the hands' is a technique for hitting an opponent in the abdomen with the backs of one's hands, and then poking his eyes. One would however never guess this from the description.

Clausnitzer and Wong, *Wing Chun Kung-Fu* (Crompton, London, 1970). An absolutely down-to-earth, fully illustrated handbook on what is probably the fastest and most effective of all means of self-defence with the fists. Wing chun is truly 'fencing with the hands' far more than savate, as its defence moves duplicate the wonderfully economical parries of western fencing. Surprisingly, the pictures illustrating techniques for use against a western boxer invariably show the boxer in south-paw stance, using a straight right, probably the most unlikely of all blows to be employed by a street brawler.

Chapter 6

The fullest accounts of all except the most recent phenomena recorded in this field are in the works of Fr Gonzalez-Quevado, already cited; and Colin Wilson, *The Occult*, already cited. Fullest information on the experiments in Russia and Eastern Europe is listed in S. and L. Schroeder, *Psychic Discoveries behind the Iron Curtain* (Prentice-Hall, New Jersey, 1971), which has the further recommendation of a totally comprehensive bibliography on the subject.

Chapter 7

For accounts of traditional fire-walking ceremonies see Sir J. G. Frazer, *The Golden Bough*, Part VII; also Harrison and Christopher, already cited. For acupuncture, see S. and L. Schroeder, *Psychic Discoveries behind the Iron Curtain*, cited elsewhere, and *Black Belt Magazine* (March 1972). Chinese practices of ritualistic self-scarification are documented in Alan J. A. Elliott, *Chinese Spirit-Medium Cults in Singapore* (Jarrold and Sons, Norwich, 1955).

Index

Richard Bach

JONATHAN LIVINGSTON SEAGULL

50p

People who make their own rules when they know they're right ... people who get a special pleasure out of doing something well (even if only for themselves) ... people who know there's more to this whole *living* thing than meets the eye: they'll be with Jonathan Seagull all the way. Others may simply escape into a delightful adventure about freedom and flight.

'Richard Bach with this book does two things.

He gives me Flight.

He makes me Young.

For both I am deeply grateful.' –

Ray Bradbury

This book, quite simply, is unique.

NOW A MAJOR FILM

Arthur C. Clarke

RENDEZVOUS WITH RAMA   40p

'Imaginative writing of the highest order ... his first major novel since that epic space odyssey *2001*' – *Sunday Express*

'There are perpetual surprises, constant evocation of the sense of wonder, and occasions of the most breathless suspense' –
        Theodore Sturgeon, *New York Times*

Rama – a metallic cylinder approaching the sun at a tremendous velocity.

Rama – first product of an alien civilization to be encountered by man.

Rama – world of technological marvels and artificial ecology.

What is its purpose in this year 2131? Who is inside it? And why?

'Consistently, continuously good' –
        Kingsley Amis, *Spectator*

PICADOR

This outstanding modern international series
now ventures into the realms of non-fiction on
subjects suited to today's inquiring minds.

Among the first titles to appear:

THE ROOTS OF COINCIDENCE/
ARTHUR KOESTLER   60p

As research into parapsychology becomes
more respectable scientifically, so the doctrines
of modern physics become more and more
'supernatural'. In this book, Arthur Koestler
discusses several syntheses of physics and
metaphysics from Pico della Mirandola to
Jung and finishes with a plea for open-
mindedness in further research and a sternly
practical indictment of both rigid materialism
and superstitious credulity. Argued in a clear
and straightforward manner, this is a fine
rambunctious essay in the punchy Koestler
tradition.

'Must be the best short summary of the
evidence for ESP as an effect deserving
investigation' – *Guardian*

PICADOR